᰾᰾᰾᰾᰾᰾

THROUGH THE GREEN FIRE

〰〰〰〰

THROUGH THE GREEN FIRE

PERSONAL ESSAYS,
PROSE POEMS AND POEMS

〰〰〰〰

James Grabill

JAMES GRABILL

HOLY COW! PRESS

Printed and bound in the United States of America.
Designed by Cats Pajamas Inc., Saint Paul, Minnesota.

This project is supported, in part, by a grant from the National Endowment for the Arts in Washington, D.C., the Outagamie Charitable Foundation, and by generous individuals.

ISBN 0-930100-60-3

Publisher's Address:

Holy Cow! Press
Post Office Box 3170
Mount Royal Station
Duluth, Minnesota 55803

Distributor's Address:

The Talman Company
131 Spring Street
Suite 201E-N
New York, New York 10012

～～～

Afterwards…
you went back
to your sky,
to the spacious heart,
to the green fire,
to the slopes,
to the trailing vines,
to the fruits,
to the air, to the stars,
to the secret sound
of the unknown springs,
to the moisture
of the conceivings in the forest,
you went back
to your origin,
to the yellow flame,
to the dark breast,
to the earth and sky of your country.

—*Pablo Neruda*
(from "Ode to the Yellow Bird")

ACKNOWLEDGEMENTS

I AM GRATEFUL to the editors of the following magazines where some of this work has been published: *The Chariton Review* ("An Earthen Night"), *Colorado Review* ("Slide Action"), *Germination*—Canada ("Crane at Lake Erie" and "In Late March the Frogs…"), *The Greenfield Review* ("Lens"), *Inroads* ("Blue Bowl," "Written During the Gulf War Bombings," "Hour," and "The Planet Moving Through Space"), *Longhouse* ("Mountain Snowfall"), *The Mythos Journal* ("City Inside the City"), *New Letters* ("Night Work"), *Northern Light*—Canada ("These Words" and "We Have Been Given Time"), *Paradox* ("Wednesday Moving Through Wednesday"), *Plazm* ("As Jets Work Through the Sky"), *Rain City Review* ("Two for the Invisible World"), *Raven Chronicles* ("Rainy Late Winter Morning…"), *The Sun* (earlier version of "Radical Nature"), *Willow Springs* ("Suddenly Tonight I Am Listening"), *The Wooster Review* ("Mule Deer"), and *Writers' Forum* ("At the Table").

Some of the poems have appeared in anthologies: "An Earthen Night" in *Crossing the River: Poets of the Western United States*, "Saturday Morning" in *Men & Women: Together & Alone*, "The Night Energy Moves in Waves" in *Nuke-Rebuke*, "Written During the Gulf War Bombings" in *Rooster Crows at Light from the Bombing*, and "Mule Deer" in *Wingbone: Poetry from Colorado*. And endless thanks to Holy Cow! editors Anthony Signorelli and Jim Perlman, to my companion Marilyn Burki, to Godparent of these essays John Bradley, and another Godparent Wendy Davis—and to teachers, editors, and friends George Kalamaras, James Tipton, Bill Tremblay, Thomas R. Smith, Allan Cooper, Bill O'Connell, Ray Gonzalez, John and Lisa Zimmerman, Casey Bush, Phil Woods, Leiv Kadmon, Diane Averill, Christopher Howell, Barbara LaMorticella, and Dan Raphael.

This book is dedicated to these fine people, to my parents and family, and to the Family of Art.

CONTENTS

A PREFACE:
THROUGH THE GREEN FIRE

THROUGH THE GREEN FIRE, forests breathe and make our breathing possible. Part of our vital energy lives in the green cooling, firing, and shielding. The green world is part of us. Saying we need it for our souls may be redundant, and yet when fiscal imperatives do their bulldozing or Bibles fly around whooing, we need to say it. Likewise, the green fire from when we were seven (or twenty) is part of us, and the forests at the edge of what we know. And where the yellow bird went, after she left. And the past and future are alive around us, sometimes the details finding us.

Green fire, of course, could not exist without blue or the river. It could not exist without the crystal-winged flies or white cars of form. A single color implies spectrums that make it. It implies diverse ways it might be seen, and contexts that spill off the canvas. This sort of interdependence might be approached in a round way, by following charged images back into reverberating memories or dreams that play into how things are now—into how certain processes can be perceived, or Gestalts intuited.

This is to say, a book might focus on themes by opening into them. It might work to integrate varieties of experience, social or psychic or perceptual. Certainly, there are a few ways of knowing, hinged on thinking, feeling, sensing, and intuiting—and shades, shadows, clarities, and energies. An essay might open a dream or memory and enter it through words asking and saying. It might pursue "what I know," but not to point back to the "I." Sometimes the point might be "what I did not know until language was approaching it," unfolding or remembering with it.

While *Through the Green Fire* has been selected (with a little help from my friends) from a much larger group of writings and has been organized logically (and I hope *symphonically*, and therefore reflective of the form of the essays themselves), I want to say the book has often felt like an entity, similar to the dream in "On the Edge of Form." That is, I dreamt the happening, but it also came to me—I wrote the essays, and yet they often seemed to be occurring to me. Where do dreams or the images in poems come from? In sharing these writings, my hope would be that their progressions and interweavings carry you into *how* you know, into your own images and process.

My hope is that this book might work like music, with rhythms and harmonics, parallels and contrapuntal shadings, improvisations and returns to the score, with cross-developments, (a)tonalities, and overtones. I hope this book moves through what it has found, that it connects, playing into ways we can know, feel, or perceive, through the earth-fire of its words.

Portland, Oregon, 1993

∾∾∾

Out from the patches of briers and blackberries,
From the memories of the bird that chanted to me...

—*Walt Whitman*

FLYING DOWN THE ROAD

PART OF US wants to fly, so there are birds. There are
finches, blue jays, cardinals, and chickadees. There are sea gulls on
the light posts of the bridge, herons standing in shallow water of the
marsh, crows talking to each other in the tops of the huge pines.
One evening after work, a small owl was calling from the grove of
pines in the park near our house. We walked toward it silently as
the air became amber. Then it flew to another tree, and then quickly
over the playing field toward the neighborhood. As she flew into
her world, we knew where we were, standing silently in the grass of
the park, not far from the river.

Part of us flies when we see an owl or duck fly. As I drove
to class the other night, I waited on an off ramp in an angled
phalanx of cars wanting to turn right toward the community college
and neighborhoods and small towns south of Portland. Red turn
signals flashed and pulsed up the incline to the intersection, and
intermittently, a car turned right into the thick rush-hour traffic
from the off-ramp as we moved closer to where we wanted to go.
I looked at the marsh near the road, and in the half-light, the blue-
amber light darkened and glowed over the water.

Suddenly three ducks rushed in from the east, turning their
bodies upright between their wings, extending their legs and feet as
they approached the water. They looked as if they were surfing
down through the air between their wings. My body surfed with
them as I watched them from my Falcon, the yellow-amber light
filming my windows with the way earth turns through steady
sunlight until reaching the edge of fullness where colors appear
from within the wholeness, the way ambers and violets show up in
people who risk the edge of their comforts, who chance approaching
the water of new language. The way ducks land, my body was
sitting upright, surfing between the wings of my thinking as I
approached the college where I would suddenly conduct class.

After finally turning right from the off-ramp of the highway,

I drove down another highway, between rolling Oregon hills, flying down through the hour before class, the hour after working at the hospital, listening to music carry our heaviness. This night The Indigo Girls, last week Paul Simon, the other month Michael Hedges—when you know you respond from deeply within your weight, from inside the solid story, you can look around sometimes, carried by speeds toward deepening sound, toward the marsh you approach with longing to be deeply alive. And the wings we are using are the way breath fills us and extends us, the way the hills vibrate with fullness. The fullness lifts, and is open beneath its form, carrying those who feel part of it through it, toward where we are going.

The way cars fly us, our perceptions of birds lift us. The way speeds report our freedom, our bodies stand up in us and lean forward between the wings of our colors. If we had been Native Americans dancing around the fire, wearing feathers down our arms and in our hair, stepping with the drums and flames through time, it might have felt like this flying through the hour down the road, moving through dusk with our humanness softly around us, and our muscles charged, responding, waiting, and our music around us. Blue jays know about muscles. When they land and hop near the sunflower seeds we scattered by the tree, they are untouchable. Their spirit radiates around them into where they can go and shows up as their blue and their cries through the afternoon air. It's the same with speeds and our colors, with our music and warm dusk coming from the distant Pacific beaches. We are almost untouchable.

Of course, sometimes deep in a turn, flares sputter and blue and red patrol lights revolve near a moment when metal and our softness struck metal and our softness. Horribly, these accidents spill toxins and drummings into silent stretches. One night in late May, I was late for work, but tried to get there, driving the Cutlass through 10:00 p.m. darkness, a little loose with wine, a little sleepy, but trying to make it. I needed to sweep my assigned area of the high school before morning, and clean the boards, pick up the trash, even though I had visited too long with writers and we had read wild poems into the winds of a community fire.

I drove down Poe Road outside Bowling Green, like a plane approaching the airport, like a duck taking a half hour to land, still hearing the rhythms of the poems, watching through the dark night for the road. Perhaps the wine had made me sleepy, but I felt awake. Suddenly as I approached an intersection where I didn't stop but the cars on the road crossing Poe did, a truck slowly pulled out in front of me! And it wasn't going to move. I was flying much too fast to avoid how slowly it pulled across the road. On both sides of Poe were ditches perhaps 10 feet deep, with sewage and rats and cattails and a sure death if I turned off the road.

I looked at the truck like a solid wall in front of me. On the side of the trailer was the name of the circus company, and an insignia, a huge lion face. I flew down Poe Road in the split second at the wall with the lion face, and the road widened darkly, glistening as if after a rain. The night air was full of Ohio spring, moist, and open. All I saw became crystalline in itself. I realized I couldn't avoid smashing into the trailer, and braked, turning the car sideways, flying toward the movie screen of the side of the truck.

It occurred to me suddenly, immensely, that this might be my last moment on earth. The Cutlass was a fine vehicle, with bucket seats that held our bodies, with sleek lines that augmented their speeds with beauty. It was dark blue the way the night sky had become dark blue with stars, and the sky opened—the moment of seeing opened wider. I watched myself unable to avoid the truck, and accepted that if I died, I wouldn't avoid it, and felt immediate acceptance of how I had tried to be a person. I had tried. In the split-second wide-open space of watching my car begin to turn, I forgave myself for shortcomings. No, shortcomings were tiny parts of gears in the motor, and the sense I had was that I had tried. I had participated and taken from others, but I had given back, too: I had been a person. From the wide-open sky, even being a person was a small thing in the massive universe that is happening. I had never *tried* to do wrong—I knew it. I experienced a deep calm and clarity, a profound release of self-limits.

I turned the car sideways, and slammed into the concrete truck, and blacked out in the blow and crumbling of metal I could still hear and yet went with. I woke as men pried my car open and I climbed out, wondering where my wife was, saying I knew Miriam had been in the passenger seat, though she was sleeping back home in the farmhouse. I walked around with the flares and flashing lights pulsing through the intersection, and then passed out, waking later in the hospital when they dropped me onto the x-ray table roughly, possibly too roughly because I smelled of the wine of the earlier poetry meeting. I hadn't been drunk. I had been clear as the night sky. My neck hurt. Terribly. A few of my ribs pushed into me, and I passed out again.

Later I woke with sand bags on either side of my head. My mother and Miriam were with me, and I deliriously talked into the air. I didn't mean to not make sense, but the words were melted, my body was numb—I thrashed and they held me down, ordering me not to move. I felt like a bird caught, trying to get loose, trying to fly off into how I used to be. Somehow we made the trip to Toledo, and soon I was sedated enough to allow the neurosurgeon a chance to drill holes into my skull for traction. If you break your neck, expect to be put into military traction, into a solidification of shape that only bones understand. But the traction felt better. The weight was off my neck, and my mind was again extended into the room and over the building. I felt sometimes I could look down at Toledo, or look down at northwest Ohio. Other times, I could only look up into the faces of my family, into Miriam's eyes, into my mother's solidness, into the faces of a number of nurses who were deeply kind to me, deeply alert.

If you break your neck trying to fly down the road, I recommend letting the doctors bolt your head to the weights. I recommend watching your father-in-law as he leads a prayer and wondering if your feet will move, but looking into the amber light of his offering. And I recommend sleeping with books near your face, asking your partner to hold one open even if you drift asleep from the chemicals to calm you down. If the St. Vincent priest enters the room, swinging incense, you can look at him in the other century and feel his endurance, whatever you believe the universe is trying to say.

But I never expected the nurses to care about me, I realized soon afterwards. I expected they'd know I tried to avoid the Vietnam War, that I had dropped out of college before finishing my degree, that I had given my common sense over to poetry and shared the wine that evening until suddenly I was driving through the night into the side of a lion. But they cared about me. The doctors worked to save me. My family visited and gave me deep support. And the nurses rubbed lotion on my back so it wouldn't dry up. A technician brought in a pair of prism glasses I could use to see people if I couldn't move my head. I lay in the bed, after the accident, ready to do whatever it took to still be a person. Cat Stevens had a song, "...if I should ever lose my legs... if I should ever lose my eyes..." He kept going. You don't think about it, you cry or talk irrationally, but you keep going, whatever you find yourself doing—you know you will keep going.

At least, that's what happened to me. Perhaps it was from the work of the neurosurgeon or from the prayers, or both, coupled with my body's insistence that the way my life could go didn't need to end—okay, I was lucky. Nothing was paralyzed. I stayed in the hospital a month, and was released with a neck splint. I learned to walk again, and soon looked down at the faces of the nurses I looked up into from the bed. I didn't expect this kind of care. I expected to be abandoned because my hair was a bit long, because I liked poetry and avoided the war. It hadn't made any difference. I got out of there, back to the farmhouse, school, and my job sweeping the floors.

This wasn't what happened to our high school's main quarterback whose neck snapped on a quarterback sneak our senior year. His body didn't move, forever. He died over the coming year, after much praying, and many car caravans of students visiting him in Columbus where he was hooked up to machines. He had been my rival for some reason, perhaps because we ran against each other for freshman class president and I beat him. I don't know why, but he didn't like me, and put me down, called me names in basketball, and one night at a bonfire walked up to me with five or so of his friends who surrounded me as he tackled me, shoving my face into the dirt. I asked him what he was doing and could feel something on my back. He said, "I'm soaping your back, you fucker."

This was at a football rally, where football players were introduced by the coaches between cheers and shouts. The bonfire blazed from the soft wood scraps heaped inside the wooden beams. It was a blazing tepee of hormones. Was there a witch nailed to the top? All I can remember is how my face was pushed into the cold dirt and thin grass, and the feeling of the guy arm-locking me, and soaping my back. When it was over, I stood up and brushed off. He shoved me, and walked off with his friends. I realized how vulnerable we are, how strong football players get, how confused, and was confused myself, abandoned by the friend I went to the bonfire with. I walked home, crying a little, and mostly repressing how I felt. I never joined the car caravans of students who visited him in the hospital three years later, but I did think of him when I was in traction. I thought of him like a brother I couldn't understand, but like an enemy too—why?

Why are we so vulnerable? Why can't we fly well enough to avoid a truck? Why are some boys so mean, and why is football so nasty? I can't believe so many men in our culture love football. I can understand how women learn to fear the power of men, as some men learn to simply force things around until they get what they want. I will never forget the nurses who connected me back to my body, and how my family stayed by me. I will never forget the wide-open moment of realizing I couldn't avoid the truck, understanding the moment might be my last, and feeling a deep calm and clarity.

When I watch finches eating sunflower seeds with the sparrows and chickadees, I feel their clarity. Some are overly aggressive, but the others move away and yet still find a way to reach the seeds. When blue jays land, they are like mountain spirits. When sea gulls fly over the river, they look hungry and beautiful, and hover impossibly in the moment before they dive toward the water or float up landing on a street lamp on the bridge.

When they fly, birds look untouchable. They are surrounded by light, and how many mid-air collisions do they have? They know how to move over the earth, over the accidents, and how to land near the highway as if our cities hadn't reached them yet. When I drive, I imagine a light around my Falcon. No, I *see* a light around my car, and drive through speeds, alert, watching, ready to brake, feeling the metals, knowing my hands are awake on the wheel, knowing I have been given another chance more than once. Sometimes the hour opens, and I watch a duck landing in the wide-open moment, and I let her fly for me: my soul flies with her over the water. When I see an accident, part of me flies into the lights asking them to be kind, my mind on the road, my soul praying for our recovery.

TWO PROSE POEMS ON QUIETNESS

I. *Crane at Lake Erie*

The white crane stops on the rocks offshore, near where a few of us swim, the waves lifting us into our bodies, the huge moon just rising, orange, in the evening, over the small shops across the bay.

The crane watches all around in the waves, where we watch, a dusk-light of our bodies around us in the air, as trees make a sky around their branches. We are quiet.

I think of how we talked for hours. Now I feel rain about to break through mountains some- where, and thick breathing wheat in the valleys of words.

In the morning, as we drive toward the highway, a crane stands perfectly still near the tall amber grass, luminous in sunlight, the crane almost invisible, like a stalk of rain, or like a pin on grandma's hat, or the scent of soap from a boy's hair, almost invisible, like something in a man, something that could fly.

II. *Blue Bowl*

A secret comes near you cannot talk to. We
live in separate mystical continents. Holding these
red stones, these red fossils, what are the red stones
holding?

The wave of his skin comes through the day-
light, the sonorous teenager sleeping in her chair, men
talking Portuguese, the woman with bright red lips
smoking back the hour, and her blue scarf...

I want to hold the secret in my arms. The
sorrow of things, needing things, wanting so much,
so many wanting, goes away, we know it goes away.
Nothing is clear as being so close we do not speak.
Or we do. The secret wants neither, perhaps, in its
red mystical hour. It stops quietly the daylight, the
way the potter made the blue bowl open.

SLIDE ACTION

A PERSONAL EXPLORATION of some of the connections between music and poetry might take the form of either. Or it might find itself in the middle of a few stories, and begin, say, in fourth grade that day our class sat in the school gymnasium in front of a man at a piano who played rhythms and intervals that we were supposed to match, tell apart, or count. We wrote our answers down on a form and then listened to an explanation of the instruments we might want to learn to play. My father and mother were musicians and we often listened to classical music, so I had some preparation for the test. When it came to instruments, I felt immediate affinity with the trombone, its sonorous tone, its plumbing and slide action. It looked like something that could make music.

A year later we were able to play some tunes and reach far enough down once in a while to hit the 6th position notes. The trombone slide is divided into seven positions, seven centers along the spine of its sound, though the seventh was clearly reserved for more advanced folks. The positions, though, weren't necessarily absolute, and often had to be slightly altered. There were secrets about how to play some of the notes so they were in tune. We learned by playing childish songs and then stepped up to Sousa marches so we could participate in parades through Bowling Green or entertain at the ice cream social in the park. The drums kept us together and stirred up our heat, which we tried to channel into the music. The publicity was thought good for the school, or the participation of so many kids was good for the community. I know we sometimes sounded as if ducks and chickens who'd lost their minds were marching with us somewhere in the ranks.

In high school, one of the more satisfying experiences I had as a trombonist was playing in a trombone trio with two other serious musicians. Both Tomi and Bob went on to major in music in college and had resonant tone, and sharp technique. I was a year behind, and studied with a trombonist at the university who emphasized lyricism and tone, breathing deeply while practicing Zen-like embouchure control. He and I went over and over scales, arpeggios, and lip slurs, and when we played duets, he usually made our sounds blend by adjusting his slide positions slightly if mine were off. He emphasized the depths of the sound, the soul, and it was a privilege to stand next to him as we practiced etudes. This teaching helped me understand a bit of what could be done with the instrument, the tonguing, blending, grace notes, held pitches, and clef transposition, say, that might be needed. In the trio, we found we could sight-read fairly intricate pieces, after scoping out the rough spots, counting out divisions of rhythm, to then blend our sounds using slight adjustments and vibrato.

Bobby had lovely vibrato, having practiced a technique using the embouchure where slight rhythmic tensing and releasing produced richly resonant held notes. There is something about a held note that doesn't have vibrato where the tone seems to flatten out and slide imperceptibly off of its mark. Perhaps it is impossible to hit a note exactly, and so vibrato is a way to approximate what is meant, to indicate a frequency by moving slightly above and below it, gently yet quickly. Embouchure-based vibrato had extra benefits, as the mouth muscles were built up and could be used for other purposes. Playing the trombone itself was actually a way of kissing the music into the world when done right, or when done sensuously, and Bobby knew how to do it.

Praising Bob's vibrato is in no way to detract from how Tomi used both mouth vibrato and slide vibrato. She was our leader and seemed older than she was. I felt she had nearly memorized our music after we played it through. She was an intelligent pianist as well, and knew ways of discussing what was happening in the music that opened it up. Bob and I were intuitive and leaned toward the lyrical, while Tomi was certainly lyrical but seemed able to divide the measures into microscopically small divisions and always seemed to know where the off-beat went. When we played energetic fugues that explored various ranges of intercellular truth and geologies of sound, we could sight-read for quite a while before someone needed to regroup—usually me. The harmonics, juxtapositions, and bodily energies propelled us with seeming spontaneity, often, and the blend was often clear.

We took our trio to contests and played for churches and school assemblies. I remember one easter when we stood in front of one of the denominations, flanked by pots of easter lilies. There was often delight in the music, and articulation, and we poured soul into it. This was so much better than Sousa or the Broadway tunes at football halftimes. Shades of emotion came from the structured spontaneity written into the music. The deep energies of sound were conjured through breath, our lips, the openness of the brass, and the vibrato.

We learned to play trombone because of, and in spite of, the structured way we were taught. If we could have studied with someone like Wynton Marsalis, say, we might have been able to improvise and to learn technique more the way we learned to speak, from having something to say that reaches out into form. Practicing lip slurs, scales, and numbered slide positions was a mathematical activity, and as it was, we tried to conform to the written music. Still, in the archetypal resonance of a fugue, I felt I knew something about freedom, and in some of the blended peaks I could see more clearly into how the trees looked on the way home.

So it was sensual, practicing our trombones, kissing the music into the air. Those who didn't play horns probably wondered how we could practice so often. In college, I played in the band, The Wooster Symphony, and a brass choir where often what was blended paralleled and eclipsed the trombone trio's sound. Brass of all ranges, played together reverently, regardingly, resulted in some of the finest experiences I have had.

But often the music felt self-conscious, or we had to count and weigh our measures to the point where the music was secondary to the group effort. The late 60s arrived, and I sensed that there was little future in trombone. Friends had guitars, and we listened constantly to Bob Dylan, Eric Anderson, Tim Buckley,

The Jefferson Airplane, The Doors, Canned Heat, Judy Collins, The Stones—on and on. This felt authentic, this kind of music, with directness, expressiveness, and primal depth. I bought an acoustic guitar from a friend for $15.00 and a few song books, and sang Neil Young and James Taylor songs that took on their own melodies and flavor since I wasn't good on the guitar and was more into the lyrics than the measures. Eventually, working on lyrics seemed like a way to practice both music and meaning, and so I put my energy into poetry, reading and writing it, even though that meant losing a way to kiss music into the air.

That was a serious loss. In playing music, there is always a connection with the instrument, and with breath. The body is surrounded by resonance or seeking. The act of playing a horn involves breathing deeply, or playing a guitar feeling with the fibers of nerves, and so the body becomes activated. In writing, the body defers to the mind and fingers, the resonances are internal and must be felt by sympathetic systems, and the connection with the air is implied. There is a time lag between writing and sharing it, or between the intervals of composing when phrases are considered and selected and the actual movement of the finished piece, whereas music works almost instantaneously as a bridge or force field one conjures and regards. Still, in writing, one factor outweighed the others for me, the possibility of being spontaneous, of suddenly uncovering a new imaginal working or associative resonance. After a while, I felt this spirit inherent in the musical use of language had dimensions that were more capable of tapping the depths of the soul than playing a single part in a musical composition. The words had voices in their vibrating and sentences had rhythm and energy, and certain deep images had long-standing resonance in the cells of the body.

In the 70s, Miriam and I often drove around, exploring Oregon when we weren't working, and found a radio station that played all kinds of progressive jazz. It was perfect for driving down the road, and for doing art at home. Rose the basset hound sat up with us in the front seat, listening and looking out the window.

We drove miles into our souls with this music, feeling the saxophone spontaneously uncovering geography behind the geography, tonal sequences behind the tones, neon back in the neon, connective bridgings behind the seeming fixed stasis of certain tunes. This was the music I wanted the words to come from—Coltrane, Sanders, Klemmer, Davis, Taylor, on and on.

What is it about the spontaneity of jazz? Certainly it has structure, deep form, and requires mastery of a couple dozen ways of looking at a scale or measure. But it seems to come from music into form, not from the page into the music. It unfolds, from deep memory into primal associations, and in that action there is expression. Implied in the expression is liberty. Of course, there is liberty in symphonies. There can be liberty even in memorizing the ticks of a clock. But in jazz there is slide action on all levels. Scales are slid through scales, harmonics through dissonance, rhythms through solitary complaints, heart through frustration or longing, and the body is activated. The emotional body is allowed to speak and explore its terrains. Mind speaks and asks, and waterfalls answer, or trails through moss-covered trees. Things open into things that open into things.

In the early 80s I attended graduate school, and one of the poets working there played improvisational piano and sax. We started to meet in the practice rooms on campus, Bill O. playing his Keith Jarrett-inspired piano and me reading jazz-inspired poems. We'd listen to the changes and progressions, Bill making new turns in the music or me jumping around in the words, and quickly found new geography in Colorado. There was a freedom, foremost, and direction. Our souls opened into the flow, and our minds into the thinking of the process we were in. This was inspired, too, by what we were studying and by the work of one of our teachers. We took our collaboration to a couple public readings, but it was never as loose and together as in the practice rooms. If only we could still cook up the jazz—but we moved to other parts of the country.

The spontaneity of jazz works in other ways than music, of course, and one way I have found to get in touch with some of it is, strangely, by playing basketball at a nearby park. I have always shot baskets for pleasure, to explore the arcs of mass through space, to think through the air into a goal, but this last spring, shooting baskets in Sellwood Park took on added meaning. After a time of working as a transcriptionist for physicians too many hours a week for my taste, I was able to cut back a little. I started shooting baskets as a way to loosen up and release my mind. There was a tree by the court towering overhead that seemed to connect to vertical dimensions of the cosmos. I found that I could look up into the tree, 30, 40 feet up into its trunk and branches, and then look back at the basket and usually feel the next shot wasn't so far and make it. I found if I shot from an off-beat, or just before or after a time when the measure would have it, I could make it more often. I learned that by forgetting I was shooting, I could do well, and if someone walked by and I tried harder, I'd usually miss.

There was improvisation in the flow of my body, in turning to shoot the ball, in not thinking but asking my body to think, in concentrating around the shot, in following it up and moving across the court. There was a liberty in finding the range, seeing the arcs through the air, sometimes before the ball was released, in surprising the ball, surprising the air, turning to shoot. There was rhythm in moving and distance that could be bridged. And clearly—inevitably—if I became too conscious of how I was shooting, I wouldn't do as well. The shot had to come from the body, which meant relaxing my mind into the open court, centering my goal on the felt hoop. It soon became instruction for how to speak, how to write, how to find the next image, by loosening the mind enough to let the body of the mind speak. How is it our words flow through us? We don't know exactly what we are going to say, and yet the words speak. The ball arcs through the air.

This was similar to what Bill and I did in the practice room, and possibly similar to playing fugues in the trombone trio. Form becomes a bearing, and yet mind opens to where it acts, from inside the occurrence, playing out from innate expression. I wish I knew how to live more of my life this way. What would it be like to loosen the mind enough to let the body of the mind speak? Perhaps many of the structures we work with in the day don't have this potential, and yet what if they do and we only need to find the release and holding and way of moving that is not distracted but in the flow, in the groove of the soul?

CITY INSIDE THE CITY

A COUPLE NIGHTS AGO I dreamt I was walking by the river near downtown Portland. There were old wooden walkways by the water, planks between piers, and docked near the shadow of an old steel bridge was a boat where a jazz group began to play. They let loose a harmonic brassy wail into the city air, calling out into the streets and shuddering some of the windows. It was surprisingly harsh, and strange they just held this sound for much longer than I'd have expected. What were they saying? The sound was full of loud sunlight. It was like light at dawn, or the light of dawn was around them. It was the beginning of the day, the beginning of their daytime concert by the river.

What was a jazz group doing, beginning a concert in the first hour of daylight? Their call was a conch sound from the river, telling people they were there, only that they were there, that the music would be going on this particular day. As I watched them, I felt they didn't need an audience for what they were doing, as the intensity of their sound said that their music propelled itself. They hadn't set up fences or gates, so they weren't going to charge people to hear them. They were confident, tuned to daylight rather than evening. They played into the open air. The river was steady. In my dream, were they calling out from the unconscious, to wake me to where they were, and possibly saying to look for other parts of the city that come into our lives this way? I woke enough to remember them, their primal sun sound, and when I woke I found myself thinking of the mystery of the city, of the downtown, the energy we call into our lives some days.

In Portland, the old buildings resonate with their jazz and buried brick streets. New buildings tower overhead with windows the size of small walls, looking out into the sky of thought, onto the abstract streets of speculations, the bridges arching over the water with streams of cars and buses weaving into the commotion and heat of our exchanges. If a few trumpets and saxophones wail out a beginning chord, dissonant and yet harmonic, somehow it is held, the buildings still reverberating in their transience, glowing neon and shouts between cars vibrating with recent nights' jams in the glint from windows and shifting traffic lights, the dark fronts of taverns and windowless dance halls still steaming with their night energy.

In the morning, cafes brew up espresso and thousands of pots of coffee. Potatoes and onions drift through the fumes. Men rummaging through trash bins reach for cans and discarded food. Crowds wait for buses, as women wearing running shoes walk quickly, their high heels in their purses. People talk, stare, look at the clock, watch down the streets as buses wheel smoothly through the traffic like sections of trains that have left their tracks in order to help us. There is action in all the waiting, parts of the sky flying through the air, teenagers moving energetically with backpacks, windows of pawn shops glowing in dark amber. Glass doors open and pull in six people at a time. Old trucks down-shift up to delivery ports, blocking traffic, as things are cooking, people moving through questions presented as answers, dresses burning red-orange and violet heat through shop windows, jewelry gleaming from inside the mountain.

In the small town in Ohio where I grew up, the downtown was a mysterious place. Its old buildings and shops spoke about what I wasn't aware of. It pulled some of us to it with its promise of surprises, the antique candy in Kiger's Drug Store with its wooden shelves ten feet up, the ladder the woman would sometimes climb, the rubber fingertips the druggist would wear when he flipped through receipts. We always laughed, thinking they were rubbers, that he had something going with the woman. Not far away, Penney's clerks sent cash payments in canisters down vacuum tubes into a small glassed-in office in back. The tubes ran up from the counters, along the ceiling, and then down into the office, and were amazingly quick, like something from a futuristic movie, and yet the building was old, the clothing was dull. There was a kind of dust in the air. Sometimes from junior high, we walked over to Whitehouse

Hamburgers and sat at the counter that circled the grill. It was hard to get a seat, as men taking breaks from the newspaper or nearby shops would go there. A bowl of chili and coke cost over a dollar, but there was something about it, a wildness, a freedom in being there.

There was energy downtown, and mystery. In the Hotel Barber Shop on Saturday perhaps a dozen or more men and boys at once sat in the old black leather chairs waiting for their numbers to be called by one of the five barbers. Nearly everyone cut his hair close to the scalp, and so it was necessary to go there every couple weeks or so, and it didn't take long once your number was called. Magazines were stacked everywhere—ones on wrestling, cars, hunting, sports—and there was a foot-high pile of Dell and Action Comics, and others I can't remember. After you climbed into the barber chair, the barber pumped the seat up a few notches, and you could look into the wall that was a huge mirror and see back into the wall behind you, which was also a mirror and reflected that image back into the other mirror, back into the other, on and on, into an infinity of rooms and fronts and backs of heads. It was a window into years, a suspension of things, a mathematics that didn't have questions to answer. The barbers talked and joked with their clients, sometimes about business or hair, or horse races or baseball. Once in a while, Gene stepped into the hotel hallway with one of the men, probably to square up a bet. People from all parts of the town came to this barbershop. You never knew what to expect.

On the surface, Bowling Green in 1961 was peaceful, a prospering post-war community, and yet beneath the surface of the world of boys there was danger, bullying, and class division. Boys from the southeast neighborhood seemed angry at others from the west. Allegiances were quickly formed and then the divisions grew. Behind the Sentinel Tribune office was a place where paperboys would pick up papers. We would fold them in a dimly lit room that was crowded and sometimes dangerous, where boys would shove someone if they wanted, or would hit him, intimidate him, or protect him. We had to ride our bikes down either of two alleys to this place, and sometimes took our chances. When there was snow, a couple older boys would take a long time making a snowball while they smoked and talked, until the snowball was nearly ice. Thrown full speed, it could nearly knock you off your bike. These were outlawed by the supervisor, but he couldn't be everywhere at once. Where did the animosities begin?—in school? In early testosterone? This isn't to say anything has changed, but there was a roughness, a wildness, where boys went, and it was part of the downtown energy adults often would never see until an actual fight broke out or someone vandalized property. Still, the possibility of having money overrode any fear of the paperboy folding room. The mysterious energy of the downtown continued working its spell.

There was a freedom downtown... with things to buy, silver dollars you could exchange dollar bills for in the elegant mahogany-trimmed lobby of The Bank of Wood County. There were cherry cokes from the fountain back in Roger's drugstore, and wild movies like *The Pit and the Pendulum* played to a full house at the Cla-zel on Saturday afternoon. This was where the collective could be found. It was like being in a dream sometimes, not quite knowing what to expect, and you felt alive. As an adult, I find I am still drawn to the downtown by the prospect of bookstores, cafes, eclectic shops, art galleries, and also by a sense of the unknown. When I moved to Portland in the early 70s, I immediately felt the city was so full of unusual lobbies and people that it was like walking through a dream. What was unknown appeared. Pieces of the psyche radiated in store windows. The unconscious pulled me into the energy to learn more about the depths of the soul, the varieties of lives and beliefs, in the exchanges of power and goods.

My first job downtown was working at the A-1 Delicatessen a block from the bus station. People from resident hotels would buy pre-made sandwiches or beer, and often we'd talk for a while. One large man who drove a caterpillar at distant construction sites lived in one of the hotels and would order two huge salami and cheese sandwiches whenever he came in. One woman whose feet never seemed to touch the floor, who spoke in a whisper, would buy three

Old English Ales and carry them back to her room. Once in a while, a slender elderly man whom I thought I recognized from old movies would lope in. He did a lot of walking around the city, and once paid me with a silver dollar that I exchanged a dollar bill for, and still have. We would talk about the summer, the heat, and cottage cheese. In July, he mostly ate cottage cheese. It was one of his secrets of health, along with the walking, and you had to believe him. These people would return often when I worked there, and other clients included a few women who worked the streets, a few transvestites, a number of people between buses, between cities, a bus driver who talked about sunflower fields in Idaho reverently, saying they were the wave of the future, and men who'd collected enough change to buy a bottle of Tokay. Once in a while, I'd give one of the wine drinkers an old sandwich we had to remove from the cooler. These people were from the city, from the collective, from inside our culture, and were part of the world those in office buildings possibly never met or imagined. They would appear sometimes out of the blue, saying things I didn't expect but often was moved by.

Being in the city with some of your senses open, with some of your soul open, I found out, can be a source of life, of stretching the soul, and accessing the energy of art. It can also be bewildering, and frightening. Downtown Portland in the 70s carried my imagination into wild realms, the way richly imagistic movies sometimes reach deeply into the psyche. But what is happening in the movie these days? It is 1991, and still the downtown pulls me toward it with its architecture and art, neon and sensuousness, and lit lobbies where stories begin that the mind picks up and carries, and dream energy is activated.

But now, too often, the downtown feels like the unconscious of the culture. What we have been ignoring will appear. Men waking from their sleep in a store doorway will step out into the streetlight. Too often, people with part of their minds too loose will walk down the sidewalk reminding us of our fears. Old trucks will drive by and we won't recognize ourselves driving. There is loose nature, dust, rain, too often the expensive restaurants with their waste and greed, banks with their coyote trickery, offices with their pyramids of people, bakeries with scent but little grain, pawn shops with their nature of taking from those who have nothing more than things, dance halls with heat and viruses, and wind from the river, silt from the clouds.

There is desire free-floating, desire in the Mercedes, desire in the shopping carts pushed by people who think they own them, desire in strawberries for breakfast in the hotel on Sunday, the desire in the City Hall basements with files of the deceased, the hidden benefits of the beef boiled in the soup, the workers boiled in the want ads, teenagers boiled in hospitals of conception, the shoppers looking for their significant others packaged and ready to go, the conformity, rebellion, the hotels speaking out blankly into the sky, distant factories punching down through the metal of lives, conveyors looking for Sunday in the back loading docks, the Gods bought and sold in galleries of objects, the money of nature, and the city of nature... the unconscious constellates when the doors close, doesn't it?, when money moves beneath the buildings. How can desire to be where money comes from aid the common good? What are the measures of that good? So much struggle and disregard undergirds success others are having. An insurance executive makes $75,000. and a man wakes in a doorway near one of the warehouses.

There is a desire some have to control the appearance of things, to surround themselves with the knowable, to "disperse" the protestors across from the City Building like a bad dream, to dispense with the extra taxes, to get rid of the red tape, and to lean heavily into the system that grants us this stay here. But the woman walking slowly in car lights, how could she be a sister? The city knows she is. The downtown reveals the sides that make up the whole. She *is* a sister. The car lights are from our culture. The system is a machine someone made to do a service. The trees are part of our souls. The red tape is a way of talking about needs. Taxes are recognition of our mutual dependence. The unconscious speaks in its downtown, and reminds us of who we also are. This is the now, each center of the city, each ignored distraction of how our goals lead us away from others and yet tie us back in, how our cars drive as if the air weren't shared.

A coffee cup touches our lips and it is every coffee cup that touches human lips. A light turned on is every light turned on by a human hand. The unique voice so indigenously who we are is every voice that has spoken on the earth, as each shoe is someone's desire, as each scent is part of the flower. Where is the congress of this kind of mysticism interpreting its common sense into mutual goals? There are few monetary goals that are not ultimately exclusive. There is little coffee that is not compromised. So the downtown jazz goes off into its culture, and the downtown taxis prowl theirs, and the dancers reveal their harmonics, the symphony meets in a sealed auditorium money unlocks, and the buses carry people into the downtown caverns.

Downtown, the bookstores overflow with philosophy and comparative culture, small cafes cook up their conversations, as the neo-Nazis cruise in the dark, and men cruise, the cars cruise, our engines burning the earth, our buildings slowing down and emptying themselves and filling up and breaking in their hours back down onto the streets of their holdings. And the knife shop gleams like a shop of crystals. The sailor bars light up like a ship's hold. The cruising crystals of an hour radio the planet from our wristwatches imported from Southeast Asia. Lost species drink in the neon and fail to appear in the daylight. A blind woman with long gray hair sits down at the table for supper. A boy who left home barters in a back booth. Dogs that work for finance companies scout the fringes of the human voice. Towering Saturnian arenas splice the gymnasium moonwalk and pressed suits of conformities. These waters filter through the reservoirs until the water is drinkable, until there is no saltwater from our bodies in the rain, until the weather is obliquely comforting and the marines return from Saudi Arabia to their jobs at the construction site. The construction site was where they always were, the jobs there, the mutual money. Downtowns know this, and disguise what is mutual. They call so many together at one time that few things could be agreed upon. They play out their jazz of harboring like an anchor in the workday, like a magnolia blossom that follows a person's speech with a question, like a chestnut tree that towers over a lost grocery cart. The downtown knows who it is and yet immediately forgets. It puts out its papers and forgets.

A while ago, Ravi Shankar performed at the Schnitzer. We bought our tickets the first week the concert was announced, realizing this was a chance to sit before one of the world's finest musicians for a few hours. The culture of India would suddenly fill the gigantic downtown auditorium with grace, spiritual yearning, deep harmonics, and earth rhythms. The concert was electrified, deeply peaceful, and time seemed to slow down and then take on ancient power, from behind the sound, from before Portland was a city. The music opened its terrains of light and regard. Ravi's sitar conjured a wholeness deep in the psyche, through the open air and breath of the room. It was an evening deep inside the evening, a city inside the city, the body deep inside our time here.

The downtown has this power in its soul. It pulls in artists and thinkers. It shows what needs to be done. It fuels exchanges of culture and ideas. Beneath all the goods and services, the soul desires wholeness, and fairness, an end to homelessness and hunger, access to education and job training. But the system that could bring this about is not in place. Many contracts still unconsciously read *1961*. The culture is still young and competitive, and the cost of living looms in the ocean clouds. Artists with vision perform a few blocks from the accounting firm. Companies pay $5.00 an hour for an honest day's work if they can get away with it. Men wake up on the street. Parks are closed to people after sundown.

RAINY LATE WINTER MORNING
IN THE RESTAURANT ON HAWTHORNE

Even in this room there is gray light of the
rain, of the breathing of canyon moss. It is a gray
with green behind it, a gray with the man in his
blue shirt by the window behind it, with the two
women talking energetically back from a coast
inside it. It is lit, the old air, as a woman in a pink
dress walks slowly through the room, past the dark
salt voices of men from the kitchen.

A light glows from the woman reading at a
small table, near the black and white '54 clock, over
the arcing radio wave lithograph chess board in
outer space made from the movement of walls
through time, and the scent of potatoes and onions,
of new coffee, and distant oranges.

There is purple, blue, and cream in a wool
sweater dashed with burgundy red, a green and
amber in people's air, as part of the low sky passes
between these buildings from 1935, 1968. A gray
from slow mines, from shore rocks, fans circling
overhead, a light from inside what it has touched
and has become, and has always been, moves
through the room and is a medium, a shaded
glowing, and quietness. Say it will be all right.

∾∾∾

Wrapped in your down bag
Starlight on your cheeks and eyelids
Your breath comes and goes
In a tiny cloud in the frosty night.
Ten thousand birds sing in the sunrise.
Ten thousand years revolve without change.
All this will never be again.

—*Kenneth Rexroth*

NEWS OF THE WHALE BEACHING

I HAVE A FRIEND whose main focus is the news, and I mean
the digested news, and the news inside the insides of the news.
Where does her information come from, I wonder, and how much
work does it take to keep up with it? She has boxes of clipped news
articles documenting the nuttiness and shifts of political values that
sweep through our public debates. She is an astute observer, an
activist loyal to people and the planet, and her writing deeply
expresses her interests in the issues of current importance.

Yet I have to think back to earlier ages, say back to 1300 or
so, and try to imagine the layer-cake earth (as Campbell referred to
it) that people perceived, with its feudal strata and its saving light
of religion. It was a time of blood-letting, superstitions, and
totalitarian control, dungeons for the bad or for those who
politically disagreed—or the gallows. And us simple folk working
our pitchforks and anvils and ovens, or getting to go to war and be
heroes (a bit like some today), or having the calling… But it was,
those times were, not violated by the glue of cultures colliding in the
center of the atom in the city business papers, or at the tip of the
pencil of the editor, or in sequences of imagery piped into our living
rooms. Of course, back then we probably wouldn't have had time to
be in our living rooms much. We would have been out with the
horses or in with the cows before collapsing and waking at dawn in
the first light for the chores before the chores and the chores.

Having turned 41, I realize that from here on out, my life
has reached the new phase available to common citizens only in
recent centuries. In 1320, I probably would have been lucky to have
lived to this late age. And I wouldn't have been able to reach for
another typing ribbon just now, or work out at the health club or see
the Friends of Jung movie this afternoon on the Gnostics. In 1320,
the Gnostics were still a jug in the ground. So the trade-off—
balancing between the stress of witnessing the big picture whether
or not we want to and the premiums of increased quality of life and

longevity—is something I accept, with heaviness, as I enter the rest of my life. It is important to know about world events and the economic struggles in other countries or our own, and yet too much can be bewildering. If we are lucky, we find further aid in understanding the dimensions of our time here—say, mysticism, astrology, or Jungian psychology—to help corral the big picture and integrate it into daily living.

Turning 41 was difficult because I felt more clearly than ever the heaviness of the trade-off, and it was difficult also for personal reasons, based on a particularly intense dream I had in my twenties. I'm unsure what year, but I think in 1977, I dreamt we were on the Oregon coast watching the thick ocean waves lift and break as they approached the beach. I wondered if any whales might be nearby when suddenly fins and then huge whale heads appeared in the waves. They were too far in, and kept coming, so many of them, sliding onto the sand. I became horrified and shouted for them to go back out, yet more and more came in. What were they doing? A few seemed to be playing and climbed onto driftwood logs, making far-flying dives into the ocean, but they still came in. It was as if they had no choice, or that their choice was to do this. I woke up in shock and wondered what it meant.

The next weekend we drove to Lincoln City on the Oregon coast where we spent long hours walking along the beach. At first we walked near the waves breaking and surging onto the shore. As always, the thunder and steady pulse of the ocean's breathing centered my own pulse and breathing, until the workweek seemed far away and the dream world close by. Soon we found ourselves walking further away from the waves, closer to the banks, perhaps guided by our basset hound who had particular affinities with washed-up and rotting beach debris and with places where the trails of people and other dogs weren't washed away.

We came to fairly large fields of driftwood timber and logs washed in over the years—manzanita, Doug fir, white pine, plywood fragments, with petrified kelp, ocean-smoothed branches, on and on. Much of the driftwood was stripped of its bark and

sanded down into living curves and slopes, and much looked
alive, with eyes, some in the form of seals or dolphins, and many
reminiscent of whales. We hopped around on the logs, appreciating
their life force and dreamtime resonance. I felt my own body there
with them, a spirit visiting their spirits, the swirls of wood reflecting
their power, the grain of the wood their inner resilience. It was a
place of transformation, of intersection of dream and waking
worlds, and also a burial ground.

After we returned to Portland, I thought the intense dream
of the whale beaching connected to finding the driftwood spirit
world. It was a private, aesthetic understanding that felt like a
closure to the seeming imperative of the dream. Then, a couple
weeks later, I was walking down the sidewalk after we had eaten
dinner at a downtown restaurant and happened to glance at the
newspaper rack. In bold headlines, I couldn't believe it: WHALES
BEACH THEMSELVES SOUTH OF FLORENCE, or something
like that. Lightning went through me. When I read the headlines,
I felt like I was standing in the middle of the sky. I was horrified,
and confused, and reread the article: 41 sperm whales beached,
only an hour's drive south from where we were in Lincoln City.

The sequence of events haunted me for months. A few
weeks or months later, we picked up Joni Mitchell's new album,
Mingus—or perhaps a year later. I can't remember the actual dates,
perhaps because the spirit connections are so prominent. The album
is a collaboration between Mitchell and Mingus where she had
written a number of lyrics for him or about him. She even wrote
lyrics for one of his famous tunes, Goodbye Porkpie Hat. Mingus
had died when they were making the album, and in the album notes
Mitchell relates some of the details surrounding his death. He was
56 when he died, and the day after that, 56 whales beached
themselves south of California. Mitchell saw meaning in the
synchronicity. The impact of both felt to her like a single event.
Was the earth mourning the loss of this great artist? Do the two
tragedies point to the even more profound disregard people at
that time generally had for the sanctity of whale life and the

contributions of artists and musicians?

The connection between 56 whales and Mingus dying at 56 raised a strange question in my mind: what could my own connection with the 41 whales mean? Something in me knows how it was back in 1320, and 41 would have been a good, long life. We have this primal memory, in the archetypal regions of our souls, and yet in that frequency I could not come up with a very good explanation. I would like to believe that 41 whales actually beaching themselves after a dream I had of that happening does not relate to when I will die. But it scares me a little, to be sure. To be sure, I have received other information through the cracks of dream energy other times and they were without personal implication. Of course, I realize the 56 whale-Mingus synchronicity is on a public scale, while my own whale beaching dream is private. Still, it looms in my mind, asking me a giant question.

After I turned 41, my partner Marilyn and I drove to Yachats, not far from Florence, for a weekend of rest. Our room overlooked the ocean, and the thundering ocean breathing worked its acusonics around us. In the day, we walked along coastal trails, and we found one forest area where hundreds of transparent-green newts crossed the path or could be seen stepping gently over the primordial forest floor, sometimes through gardens of mushrooms and low-hanging moss, beneath licheny trees and rocks, near regions of open earth and scent, with a faint mist in the ocean air. The newts were so gentle and their frequencies quickly took us back in.

We drove further down the coast, looking for more colonies of mushrooms along a couple more trails, until we realized we were almost in Florence. It occurred to me that we might want to go south of Florence to where the whales had beached themselves. We found a state park and walked across great, wind-crazed dunes. The wind was intense and nearly blew us over the way it does in the foothills in Colorado sometimes, but we continued over a few more giant dunes and then could see the ocean—perhaps a mile or more away. Dimensions were difficult to grasp, as they are often at the ocean.

44

I wanted to walk all the way to the ocean, but it was late in the afternoon, perhaps 45 minutes before dark, and a wall of rain was darkly gliding toward us over the ocean. So we walked back toward the car, and ran, leaping down a couple of the dunes with the wind at our backs! The drive back up Highway 101, over the old stone and steel bridges and through the small coastal towns was reviving. Soon we were driving in the night through thick rain, tremendously relieved we had returned when we did.

How did this visit to the land where the 41 whales had died speak to the memory of the dream? In my notebook, I jotted down the overriding sense of the place: "vast distances, giant dunes, dunes like in the middle east?, dunes like long periods in our lives?, and still more distance to the actual beach, to the spot of the beaching and the spirit transformation sites..." It could be that this sense of distance was a good sign for me personally. On the other hand, the dunes were inhospitable and some people in dune buggies had been there earlier in the weekend so their tracks were etched in all over the central dunes in the park. Was it even more like the Middle East than I wanted to imagine, as hundreds of thousands of soldiers drove their tanks and armored cars into the showdown there? And once in a while, the dunes were whale-shaped, I felt, and heavy, burying something. Gray wood broke out of the sand like whale bones at the foot of a couple dunes. There were also a few purple flowers in the middle of all the dune-buggied grooves—one purple flower bloomed in the middle of nothing but sand that seemed so transient in the heavy wind, but it wasn't phased by the transience. It was blooming anyway, at the beginning of December, in a valley between two dunes.

I know we could have planned a hike to the actual site of the beaching if we had thought ahead, and yet this spontaneous visit to Florence was perhaps in keeping with the spirit that gave the dream. I want to pursue the beaching further another time when it calls, or perhaps some other ocean dream will lead in another direction. News from these realms sometimes takes months, or years, to reach part of its words. And how often does it speak so quietly it is silent?

As a dreamer, I ask for guidance, and for more information, but the chronology is confused and the symbols live in their coastal realms where distances are not easily discerned, where their personal meaning shifts and curves with the driftwood and thundering ocean floors.

(1991)

AS JETS WORK
THROUGH THE SKY

How do jets unwind from their spools?
In the heat behind them, Navajo rugs burst into
flames. All our woven hair. The furnace of stars a
blue clay bowl is pulled from.

Effortlessly the celery carries the sun in its
leaves. Water knows its descent through blue-lit
air, moss on limbs of the sequoia, ocean moss in
tiniest parts of breath.

A wind in solid things opposes their
change, or causes it. A woman cuts into jade in
Thailand, the way light falls over East Cherry,
changed a few blocks. The minute carving.

And behind the jets, the seabird's floating
teeth in starlight eat at the earth-body, eating it
into shape. In front of the jets, in the curve of
cheekbones and scarlet-lit yards, or blue heights
thick in the coves, a cool heat wavers and warns
and longs.

WRITTEN DURING
THE GULF WAR BOMBINGS

What is the answer to the team
of adrenaline? When the world
collapses, what is its flag?

What is the answer to a bullet
of congress, to a family
of rations, to the lost policy?

The time it would take has left
the earth, the time has been buried
in its time, the buried in the buried?

What is the answer to the storm of dust?
What is the dust that pours
part of its river over a body?

Who is counting, and who will remember?
When the scope-to-scope firing
plows through living bearings,

when the eye-to-eye combat
sparks up in its tanks of heat,
when the hearings of each eye

head off toward separate corners
of sand, when the thick oil
drenches the inside of the wave,

who will be shouting for more
and who will keep forgetting
and flying, when the holsters

sling back toward an infinity
of blocked-in bunkers, back
in the shells of exploding light's

skin, the final shouts and cries
of the bunker, the needle-threads
of shouts, when the body swerves

and the heat-metals pump through
thoracic forests, who is going to forget
and who will begin to grieve?

HOUR

At the speed of light
in the soul, a river
stops progressing in how it moves
always like the green grass
growing and dying back,
the thick branches of earthy strength
heavy with earth scent and trying.
The river is like its rocks,
a constant flow and waiting,
at a certain depth, and yet
in the hour of things
how much is lost and carried away?
Even the way we can speak
is carried off; even the people
who didn't come to the meeting
can't be reached.
The cool air that quenches a few nights,
whose gasoline was that, white
in the wings of cranes?
Lives do not repeat themselves,
do they?, not at this depth
of reconvergence, not with this much
green grass, thick green vines,
and immense green trees.
Not in the seed deep in the hour,
the only hour, the room and its only
people, and the persons you can see
looking out, from all corners
at their people, whose trucks
you can see on the roads,
whose faces open the root
word sometimes in a cafe.

ON THE EDGE OF FORM

In space, in the center, roaring
with vacuum and form,
planets wheel the churning
suns around in coves.

SOMETIMES A WEEKEND away from home will loosen
energies that hold things in place. Emotions submerged in the
workweek may find room to reverberate. Questions might lead
to further turns of the road. Sometimes the horizon will shift to a
larger span of time, especially if the destination is the mountains
or the coast.

For me, the Oregon coast opens elemental resonances.
The half-submerged coastal rock helps me with primal emotions.
The roar of the waves massages the static from my body. The sea
caves in my chest and abdomen listen down into the water to where
sea lions are diving. In tide pools, anemones sway back into the
brain of the ocean flower as the water in the cells of my body lifts
toward the buoyant thundering tons of ocean water.

On the beach, the dunes and grasses move distances back
so that walking takes longer. Light fractured in the breaking waves
peppers the wind with its salt bite. Or on calmer days the light
floods the beach for hours and then slowly pulls away in a great
wave, leaving behind the evening.

Each time the coast is different. The surging water gives its
primal answer. Each time its cohesion curves the air differently.
And certain mornings of fog linger half in the world of form and
half in the waking dreamscape, where sometimes New York doesn't
seem so far away or a friend in a distant room will feel nearby.

One morning in thick fog I ran along the coast in Newport
and sometimes had the sensation my body was transported into
how some of our words live on in future times. It was an indistinct
feeling, threaded invisibly yet palpably by laser outlines. And faces

came through and re-entered the fog as my body breathed through all its cells into the new body I kept entering. At one point I prayed to the ocean for guidance and looked up to see a flock of brown pelicans flying in a line close to the shore, closer than they usually get, their sense of space like mine confused by the fog. I don't think they saw me, and quickly they were gone.

Sleeping in a motel on the ocean side of Highway 101 is almost always calming. The steady, rhythmic roar of waves is the earth breathing. In the depths offshore, whales are passing. And sometimes in the early morning, intense dreams will slide into form through some new opening.

One night recently we stayed in an Arch Cape house we rented through a classified ad in the newspaper. It sounded rustic enough in the description, but the room where we slept was near the washer and dryer, and the heater didn't work. The walls were nearly blank, with little art or sea relics to reflect the energy of the small ocean cove we could hear and feel around us. It was a cool October night, and so we bundled up in the bed to keep warm. I was extremely tired from the workweek and off balance by the lack of heat and aesthetics, but maybe that stirred up dream energy.

Early in the morning I dreamt I was in my hometown a few blocks from my parents' house, close but further than I was allowed to go as a child. I stood on the avenue with a friend with a goatee and wanted to communicate. I looked up into the night sky, thinking there might be something to see that we could talk about metaphorically, and saw the nearly half moon with a few intense planets or stars near it. We started talking about how the particular configuration seemed unusually meaningful.

Just then from the north a huge presence that filled part of the sky rolled in. It was like a wheel of laser energy and round centers moving in rings and spiral arcs that seemed to come from another dimension. It seemed to roll across the sky and didn't get larger as it approached, and so it wasn't adhering to lines of perspective the way something in the three dimensions of the world would appear. Perhaps it came from inside where we were.

It rolled out of the north and stopped overhead, and seemed to be looking down at us. I asked it immediately, "What do you want?" The voice seemed to come from deep inside my chest. I was worried it wanted to do something, that it wanted something. What was it? The presence waited a moment and then glowed and dissolved into a peaceful white light through mist. Like a blessing.

Perhaps something in my fear caused it to tone down its lasery circling geometry, and it pulled back behind a veil which smoothly dispersed its light. I woke, and was unable to get back to sleep. The presence seemed to have had a kindness. It realized from my question that I needed reassurance.

When it rolled across the sky, it never changed size. It seemed to come from inside the universe. It felt like a foundational presence and didn't seem otherworldly. Still, I had been afraid. It was magnificent, and my friend and I were just two men on the street in front of middle class houses. What could we offer it? What was it saying?

I got up early that morning, put on running clothes, and started for the beach. A cool morning fog obscured the nearby distances. It was impossible to see the end of the beach, though I knew we were on a cove. I ran south, the roaring of waves on my right, dreamlike shapes of buildings on my left. Occasionally in front of me I could see two people walking, surrounded by the pure space of their time here. I felt we were spirits moving along the edge of form. I ran into the light in front of me that filled all my body. When I passed close to sea gulls I felt as if I were a white bird with giant wings in the fog calmly carrying me, not to disturb them.

Maybe a mile along the shore I could see I was approaching massive ocean rock. I ran on the surface of this planet until I came to water and had to turn around, back into the gray fields of my time here, running into the cool ocean breath I love.

Later, I tried to draw the presence. It was spherical and lasery, yet flat. Part of it was visualized movement, and so the drawing couldn't begin to show how it was. And the way it shifted into misty light—how could I describe the way it felt like an answer to my question? Did it say to look for it in the way light comes to earth, or in the way we are able to see?

What did it want? Its geometry seemed intelligent, to have come from mind. Did it say to feel the mind of the light that reaches the earth? The way it responded to my fear was to soften and disperse, to enter the natural world. When it did that, it felt kind. Did it answer that this kindness can be felt in the light of the world, that the world is a manifestation of this regard, or we can learn to perceive it that way sometimes if we know to try?

In the fog, as people come into view, they usually look like a kind species, when they have enough space, when they are close to the ocean. What is it we have to offer—kindness, know-how, regard? But how difficult it is in this culture, with the confusions of money and power, the lapses of deeper meaning, and the tremendous problems of our time.

THE PLANET MOVING THROUGH SPACE

IN EARLY NOVEMBER, the days seem to be more submerged. In the morning before work, we move through the house, turning on lights as we go. Then, at the end of the workday, it is dusk, and evening already. Soon the ocean rains lower the Pacific Northwest sky. Even the middle of the day seems to be sinking closer to solid earth and the solidness of things.

With the sky close and impenetrable, leaves give off more light. The color of someone's hair is more noticeable near the metallic blue-silver windows of the new medical building. Incense lit at home near bedtime uncoils and swells through the leaves of air forced up its trunks and branches from the basement furnace. There is a hunger that things have from us, that they wait in, at the edge of our heat.

As the ceiling of the sky grows thicker, the people near us in rooms move more noticeably. Meeting up with a friend unexpectedly on the sidewalk feels more synchronous. More meetings are held. More dreams are consulted, with or without the dreamer's asking. What is the goal of society? We feel like deciding. We feel like buying things, to be able to take home some of the earth's meaning. We look for gifts we can give. Chairs and tables speak more clearly into our bodies. This happens as the year slowly falls from some of its sky, as days close more early, as the doors are colder.

It is a huge process, the planet moving through space, the sun coming from the nearby world. When I grew up in Ohio, we knew that snow wasn't far away, that light would crystallize from inside the rain, that the mud would stop sliding under our steps, and day would gather itself back under the silence that kept it. In Oregon, though, the rain continues looking for its ferns and huge ocean firs. The darkness of its work deepens, and sometimes heaviness of the body becomes aligned, closer to our trunks, back in the hours.

When I feel this heaviness in my body, I know it is different than depression. It pulls me closer to the moss and old leaves. I like to drink coffee in a lit cafe as the rain is falling. With depression, I feel myself going numb, disconnecting. The shadow body works its flames, and my chest goes hollow. If I feel the rain falling, my empty body echoes.

Heaviness, though, like depression, can lead to slowdowns at work. Business seems like distraction. The shadow moves closer to the lunch table, knowing how much is out of view, how much we haven't been able to do, how deeply others leave our lives sometimes. It is close to the chair, close to the door, close to the suitcoat, asking its half-buried questions.

Heaviness isn't depression, though. Its shadow doesn't enter the body to show us how insubstantial we are, judging us hollow over and over. But it does sense the lunch room, like a lit boat, passing steadily through its time. The neon of shop windows writes slow words into its late afternoon. The warmth of the room is part of that writing. It says we work hard, and have so much more to do. It says the rain is falling through this chance corona of space.

In depression, the shadow doesn't have to speak, since it has more body. Its failure to pronounce its sentence makes us search for questions. Why haven't I been a better person? Why can't I remember more? The shadow knows why. It is never satisfied. It never has enough body.

Depression unhooks the "I," as the body watches? Depression is unacknowledged grief? Heaviness weighs down, but leaves the body solid? Heaviness knows grief of so much trying, so much living. Both, however, can unhook the day and remind us how we will die from all we loved or worked on, from daylight and even the sound of the rain at night. Both, too, if we walk them far enough, sometimes fall inside out in sunlight, into the opening of light in the day without solidness or bound until the light is gone, forever, in the void.

From there, look suddenly at a squirrel, your hands, or piece of bread. Look at the neighbor walking past the house. To think life formed in this way, with these breaths, in this part of the solar system. These legs, this scent of old wood, this clay plate, these long fir needles.

I know we move through pain, each as he learns to, as he is ready. But why does heaviness in others so often feel like depression to me? Why do I want to solve the question? I feel powerless too often next to a friend's darkness. Sometimes, in fact, I feel I may have caused it, as I know the love I haven't given. My heaviness hollows out, listening to the wind in another's suffering, feeling my own remorse, knowing too well the shame. My mother is sick on the living room couch. I want to help her, but she tells me to leave her alone. How old was I?

There is a way to see health in dark energy. I haven't learned the lesson. What am I asking now? How can I trust another's suffering? I know that part of us is this half-lit rain. I know how hard it is sometimes to simply wake in the morning when the earth is heavy. I know how we can appear more vividly to one another in November, and how the room is passing steadily through the world it finds.

The teacher asks how we can be close if we aren't sad. But why do I long with all my heart for the world to be all right, for those close to me not to be sad? How can I process space for our closeness? This unfinished longing, what does it want? Our heat bends as the month submerges a little more, a little more. What is the gift that can speak to that? Do the colored scarves in small shops know what to say? Does food given for another's hunger ask where the rest of the food is, why we are so slow, why the trucks are two days late?

I light incense and sit a while longer, before joining my lover in our bed, where we will sleep in our own worlds the rest of the night.

THREE CHANTS AFTER DARK

I. *An Earthen Night*

Oxygen drinks down into the flames
of the houses and rooms set back
in electric lights with people talking.

The cool night surges back after work
into hard floors and sheets of TV light
through the sound of ice in the glasses.

Oxygen of the fields buried in streets
shimmers, back into cooling engines, down
from new speeds and ultraviolet clouds

of birth pulsing invisibly from red hospitals,
tender meat smells swelling over the river
and drinking down railroads with thoughts

where cups pile up, and strangers carrying
part of us disguised at the door,
and identity buried in hotel lobbies

and duties that have been waiting
for us to come here, broken into headlights
shining back, toward the turning over

of last century, with a few gulls
over crystal vaults of big buildings,
distant gray whales diving through

blue lights in the water, listening
to pouring walls of fish in their waves,
squids shooting out into black flocks

of water, sand crabs on dunes
in the waves of breath, the bears
sleeping, pain breaking off bodies

forgetting where they began, the night
surging down the horns of each worm,
down the tiny breastbones of spiders

and fish masks echoing, cat bones
where ice forms, where a brother walks
with the negligee of dusk gliding

ahead of him, the green wheat rising
behind him with insect spines
darting, in the human shaded sound

of our voices, and the cool night
drinking down the spiral halls
of plants and the sax working.

II. *Mule Deer*

In these foothills I cannot see them.
They survived the blizzard together
and will appear one night
when we do not expect them.
Down the lines of sight,
I long to see their freedom.
I want them to leap, unlike any others,
through the grasses and brush.

When I love another person,
I long for the sudden hours
of freedom. Moonlight on the snow
appears one night. When I see a deer
in hills nobody owns, I look for the others
no one has seen. They learn by moving together,
listening to shifts of breath in the wind,
standing invisibly with the limbs of sumac,
waiting like dark flowers of moss and bark.
I do not want to hurt anything, anybody,
and I do not want to be hurt, and I hear the wind
down below, and the water and the breathing.

When things blink, the deer run higher,
when the dogs of the stars blink.
Driving home from work one night
I see mule deer, wild, feeding
with cows in a field. I see dogs
on porches, and houses on the hills.
I want to be with those I love.

III. *Suddenly Tonight I Am Listening*

Tonight the rain enters wood through the roots.
Tonight the light-bodies we become sit down in our bodies.
Tonight in their ocean, dolphins and sojourns and maples,
    listening.
Tonight the cinnamon and curry and milk that is asking.
Tonight as low rumblings, as water on dream streets,
    as rain walking in a man or woman leading us.
Tonight amber from oats and rustling harbors of wind,
    and clouds of more world about to form.
Tonight the blue jay back in her nest, and her nest
    in our bones through which the night sky passes.
Tonight a horse breathing behind us, luminous, vanishing,
    as in their mountain, feathers are speaking.
A bird's stratospheres in the centers of air know.
Fire flashes from old camps folded in the stones
    holding mind, trees planting the earth
    between stars as between cells.
Tonight the wood carries rains through the sky
    of its body, into leaves and mind.
As all words form again when any is said.

৵৵৵

The poet knows that he speaks adequately
then only when he speaks somewhat wildly,
or "with the flower of the mind"… As the
traveller who has lost his way throws his reins
on his horse's neck and trusts to the instinct
of the animal to find his road, so must we do
with the divine animal that carries us through
the world.

—*R.W. Emerson*

৵৵৵

The male is not less the soul nor more.

—*Walt Whitman*

A DREAM WITH FLIES

IN A RECENT DREAM, I was counseling with a wise woman
friend about the meaning of the *feminine.* The room was crowded,
the light was dusty, and some kind of preparation was going on.
A women's group was getting ready to leave for a weekend retreat
at the coast. My friend was going to serve as a facilitator there, and
she tried to talk to me as she also carried on a conversation with one
of the more energetic women who moved supplies from the kitchen
into the living room where we were. My friend suddenly had
rollers in her hair, and then there were more boxes and bags in the
room. I tried to ask about the smoothness of the brush stroke in an
ink painting on the wall but again we were interrupted. I tried to
keep my mind fixed on my purpose, but we were disturbed,
distracted, and the room itself kept changing.

I knew the women's retreat would be a mysterious and
magical gathering. If only I could go, if only I could have the
background I'd need to pass as a member of the group, and yet
I knew all I could do was wait to ask my questions. The woman
carrying the material into the room brought in a few baggies of
important items, including food and certain meditation aids, the
latter interesting me immensely. I could imagine there were
luminous jewels or organic shells, or small intricately carved images,
so I watched as my friend checked on the contents of one of the
baggies—flies. Three half-dazed flies. She assessed their condition
and nodded, and I looked on in disbelief. The jewels were flies?!

One of the flies fell off the aluminum TV tray into the shag
carpet. I bent down to help find it, knowing it was needed, though
still confused how it could be important. The fly had a bit of energy,
and as I looked closer it was a tiny fly-sized monkey climbing up a
thread back to the top of the TV tray. How could I ever ask about
the mysteries, about the retreat? There was so much distraction in
the room that I hoped my friend would suggest we leave the room
and go for a walk where we could talk together in peace. She

looked at me, paused, and then told me we should go for a walk. Relieved, I agreed, and then woke up.

What a noisy dream, with so much distraction, and yet there was a lot of preparatory work in what was going on, a gathering together of materials. Though I wanted to converse, I felt relaxed with my friend, who was obviously not concerned about appearances, with the way the room was disorganized, with the Sears TV tray, her hair in curlers, the venetian blinds without drapes. I usually think of her as earthy and stunning, self-contained and prepared—how much of the clutter of the dream was I bringing in with my questions? I did see the brush stroke on the wall hanging, with its fluidity that was spontaneous and yet controlled, vivid and yet softened by the impressions of the individual brush hairs. Perhaps there was no question about it, as it stood for what it was, generated at a moment of knowing that took action and yet received it. It seemed to approach the shape it took and was the result of study as well as the fluidity of inner reaching.

But, of course, the flies bothered me. Why were they treated so carefully, and how would they be used? When my friend handled them, she held them gently to make sure they were still alive and then placed them back into the baggie. In the dream, I had been certain there would have been jewels, perhaps rubies, or quartz crystals—but flies?

In his later writings, Mark Twain wrestled with ways people think about God. What possible wisdom was there in epidemics that randomly took human lives, especially the lives of children? And how could a loving God have created the carriers of many of those diseases, the flies?—

> There is much inconsistency concerning the fly. In all ages he has
> not had a friend, there has never been a person in the earth who
> could have been persuaded to intervene between him and
> extermination; yet billions of persons have excused the Hand
> that made him—and this without a blush. Would they have
> excused a Man in the same circumstances, a man positively
> known to have invented the fly?... We cannot understand the

moral lapse that was able to render possible the conceiving and
the consummation of this squalid and malevolent creation.

Because flies feast on death and randomly spread disease, Twain felt
their presence in creation reflected the "application of pure
intelligence, morals not being concerned" ("Thoughts of God").

Certainly people and flies are mutually better off if they
keep their distance from one another. In "The Fly," Galway Kinnell
tries to make a kind of soul-peace:

> The fly
> I've just brushed
> from my face keeps buzzing
> about me, flesh-
> eater
> starved for the soul.
>
> One day I may learn to suffer
> his mizzling, sporadic stroll over eyelid and cheek,
> even seize on his burnt
> singing with love.

The fly carries with it an insistence, a random activity, and a hunger
for the soul itself. It is the unconscious messenger of what we don't
want to face, perhaps, the leveler of remains. The fly is like the
hunger of the soil for its animals and people, like an ancient curse,
or at least an energy that does not have our best interests in mind.

What possible use would flies be for the women's retreat?
In the dream, the flies were docile, even tamed. The one that fell
on the floor became a monkey, perhaps pointing to our own
monkey-generated bodies. Controlling this power could be quite
useful, or at least recognizing it, seeing it as part of the ways things
go. But beyond that, the flies were in the baggie. Were they some
kind of food?

As a man having the dream, I had to wonder if the flies
were a food for the frog part of my psyche, if, as in the fairy tale,
I was still the raw material of myself in some way—before the

princess threw me against the wall and I turned into a man. To be sure, they didn't whet my appetite, and I was disappointed; but how much of daily life is like that? I think of the annoying, tedious details at work, the numbers in the bank account that keep cancelling out possibilities, the way the side of my car thunked and screeled as I scraped another car's bumper by the coffee shop, the way ants have been tunneling into our kitchen, the way the clothing fades, the disagreement surfaces, the socks wear through, the light in the living room hangs drably in the afternoon sometimes. This kind of material, maybe, is food for the human frog, in how it feeds our strange hunger for fly energy?

Where do the flies in rooms come from? And why do they show up suddenly, buzzing, like agitated pieces of topsoil? What could we learn from their presence? Kinnell contrasts the fly with a bee:

> The bee is beautiful.
> She is the fleur-de-lys in the flesh.
> She has a tuft of the sun on her back.
> She brings sexual love to the narcissus flower.
> She sings of fulfillment only
> and stings and dies.
> And everything she ever touches
> is opening! opening!
>
> And yet we say our last goodbye
> to the fly last,
> the flesh-fly last,
> the absolute last,
> the naked dirty reality of him last.

The gender designations Kinnell chose certainly aren't necessarily the way things go in the worlds of bees and flies, and yet there might be a point well taken in that fly energy more clearly connects to the "absolute last" or even the dirtiness of "reality" than bee energy. Where there are blossoms, bees are working, but where there is garbage, shit, remains, the flies are working, though of course some flies also attend blossoms.

As far as our sense of moral rightness, bees would seem to have quite a jump on flies. Bees seem to have a more honorable purpose. And yet doesn't part of the soil need to fly up out of itself, to regulate itself? Aren't the bodies of flies wiry crystallizations of one of the ways soil becomes itself?

In the dream, the flies, then, perhaps were crystals of a certain kind. They were unexpected, part of the energy in the soil that roots feed out of. In our moral hierarchies, they are near the bottom of the chart. Yet their wisdom is dailiness, but deeper than that, primordial survival, futuristic, and from the point of view of the soil, necessary. How are they different from the microorganisms in our intestines, say? They seem drawn to what intestines produce. They seem drawn wildly through the air where they are trapped in rooms that perhaps seem as randomly constructed to them as their flying appears to us.

I don't know what I am unable to face, generally, but I know I am likely to fail to notice valuable details wherever I go. What romanticized generalizations do I carry in with me when I meet with a female who teaches me or attracts me? What beauties do I ascribe to the earth without seeing the actual ways spirit is working through matter? (Or is it matter emanating from spirit?) I want to see wholeness in people, wholeness in the earth. In the dream, the flies were part of a learning that would go on at the retreat. They knew what they were doing. And my friend (anima) had a sympathetic handle on their power.

WE HAVE BEEN GIVEN TIME

Saturday, an afternoon in the century,
where time has escaped between the houses
in a first power, and those we carry inside us
are a snow rising up in the trees of moonlight,
moonlight of an afternoon, where months pass
in galaxies overhead.
                              Unlike any other,
this time here, thoroughly itself,
and we are here by an easing up
of the weight, allowing us this chance
to breathe and walk around and do
a few things. If we can't love now,
then when?
                    We know the blue mountain light,
boulder fields in their armada of gravity,
health and illness, this plant life
and sleep of mammals, thoroughly wind
still the first wind, the light
still its first time. When we die,
will it seem as if nothing happened,
as if we were never holding
each other?
                    It is as if we could survive
in the silence of Bach or B.B. King,
giving ourselves to grace when it happens,
then the way light from central Europe
falls onto the downtown Portland buildings,
luminous, from another time, and yet here,
exactly, and the weight lifts for a while,
and it is Saturday.

MORNINGS

I. *Night Work*

Late in the morning and still asleep.
And still asleep at twelve noon.
And still asleep in the blue fog.
And still asleep in the sun's wheat.
And still asleep in the hum of engines.
And still asleep in the cold melon.

Late in the evening and still asleep.
Awake but asleep in the moving sound.
Awake but asleep in the telephone sky.
Awake but asleep in the clear talk.
And still asleep moving the leaves.
And still asleep with the icy peaks.
And still asleep with lights at sea.

II. *At the Table*

You have never been here before
in this part of your house,
you tell someone. Then you wake

alone, and move slowly through
the rooms of a music you have
gathered around you, like other

people you know. You feel your home
stretched out around you for miles
in the presence of men and women

you care for. Some you haven't met.
Then you tighten into your muscles
and skin, into the shape of a man.

You sit at the table, suddenly
like one of the grandfathers,
in the ancient shape.

III. *These Words*

A word is its own revision.
A previous word is always
revising a previous word,
and a future word guiding it
through a canyon, the word
spoken by a horse rider in 1874
near an anvil, by a woman
in Hanover after insurrection
installed a new legal tender,
whispered at a small gathering
of great aunts of a grandmother
and by a boy near the Mississippi River
of his father's account,
or by a mother whose baby was born,
or by someone unborn in someone else.
A sea wind comes between us.
A slanted pine shadow.
Clearly we are not new.

IV. *Saturday Morning*

As we wake,
you touch me,
your lips on my shoulder.
I move my hands
over your back
and we hold each other,
in an hour that no one
can take away.

In longing, holding you,
I almost cannot bear
the passion I feel
waking this morning,
in the second
half of our lives,
on an earth that sometimes
gives us a place to be calm
and humanly delicate.

When a morning like this
is given, nothing
can take it away.

HUGGING

SATURDAY MORNING, the early sun and blue sky, the full
spring around us—I could have slept in, but words had begun
inside me, words about hugging… I heard, or thought, "hugging is
a way to feel the soul *through* the body." The image was clear.
While our bodies are not distinct from the soul, at the same time
they are the instruments of our soul, and other levels play in—light,
energy current—surrounding us and flowing through, as we hug.

Some people hug with deeply nurturing regard, some
people as if they are asking whether you like them. Some transfer
intimacy or solace from other relationships into their hugs.
Sometimes when I hug someone I have the distinct sense we are
coming from distant cities, and perhaps are ambassadors at the door
of the conference room; in men's groups sometimes it is like that.
With friends, there is some kind of transfer from family. There is
a sense that we are here for one another, and if one person is in
trouble, the others will be there for her. Of course, some of the
deepest hugs recognize that we are two people on earth, given this
chance here, having been together or just now getting together, in
the remarkable instance of life here, in the uniqueness of our being
together, in the deep connection we feel for each other.

As I think about hugging, my body is alert, bringing back
images and senses. I mean, think of the major hugs in our lives.
What a potentially rich energy our bodies have in them from all the
arms and shoulders and human light and breasts and kisses on the
face. Sometimes on Saturday morning we can wake, and our skin
and muscles from deep in the bed will be remembering.

Hugging is a way to feel soul through the body. Our soul is
activated, and the other person's soul, and there is a light, a warmth,
shelter, a union and individuality, the current flowing. When I have
felt this, sometimes the moment has marked thresholds, growth, or
returns. I think of one night Marilyn and I walked through Fort
Collins, talking and looking at the old cottonwoods in January,

noting houses that spun us into stories or that had stained glass or vivid paintings we could see on the living room walls or wind chimes playing a distant European chord, or we noticed secret windows, old cars, luminous branches, or architecture saying a few things.

The winter night was full of energy, as was our walking, and the full moon illuminated the pines and new snow and our bodies. We stopped a few yards from an intersection of two quiet streets, under the moonlight, under tall pines, and hugged, kissing, deeply, from all we were, so openly, so connected. The hug and kiss transported both of us profoundly. We talk about it as the "famous kiss." How can something like this be described? We had thick coats on, and the air was cool but charged. The moonlight was primal. We were in the primal night of each other, in deep caring, in our mid 30s; and in the moonlight through the pines, holding each other, we experienced a union, a wide-open clarity, and grounding. That night, we didn't mention the kiss as we continued walking, but later we agreed it was unlike anything either of us had experienced before.

What is it about an embrace of that magnitude? Certainly the energy of our communication had loosened us, and our mutual attraction had primed us. I think of images from an early poem by Robert Bly, "Looking into a Face":

> Conversation brings us so close! Opening
> The surfs of the body,
> Bringing fish up near the sun...
>
> I have risen to a body
> Not yet born,
> Existing like a light around the body,
> Through which the body moves like a sliding moon.

There is a power in the surfs—full of memories and insights and other kinds of fish—an actualization, that fills a deep conversation. There are images and impulses of who we are or what we value that

73

rise close to where the sun of the other person enters the surf that is the energy around us. Activation and clarity can lead to a connection, past all thinking, that two bodies holding each other can transmute through senses into mutual grace.

When we close our eyes, sometimes we can see some of the fish. Where this goes on might be thought of as an inner womb, as Meinrad Craighead describes, a place with dreams painted on the walls. After moving back to New Mexico, she experienced a profound synchronization between her inner images and the land: "I found the land which matched my interior landscape. The door separating inside and outside opened. What my eyes saw meshed with images I carried inside my body. Pictures painted on the walls of my womb began to emerge" (from *The Feminist Mystic*). This kind of merging can happen with the land or with another person. Both Craighead and Bly envision a womb energy, a containing individuality, that makes mystical union possible, and that results in a door opening, or the surfs opening, to the point where a mystical birth is possible. What is born is art work, conversation, but more than that—in Bly's poem, the womb is a "body not yet born, existing like a light around the body," through which his actual body emerges, through which his actual Soul is his body emerging. Perhaps a "famous kiss" opens in a similar way, the two people energized, held by a light around them, through which they move.

So a kiss in the moonlight on a magical night can become a bearing, a peak moment of knowing, bearing us into our lives. We feel contained, deeply home, and then opened, granted our lives in the other's arms. Perhaps only a lover's embrace (or a particular place's embrace) can open the door that separates inside and outside, and the surf is full of life force, nurturing, desire, comforting, waking… And yet I can remember other remarkable hugs, certainly from my mother and father back in the old times before I could talk or before I could leave the house on my own. Those were mythic hugs, so close to the source of life, hugs after walking a few steps, hugs after waking in the morning, hugs when crying, hugs where the body is lifted up into giant arms. We carry the *mythos* of those hugs wherever we go, don't we? Perhaps a source of disappointment in the world is how daily events do not share the unconditional love of those hugs, but rather surround us with separations and competitions. If we could ever get past our disappointment, would it be possible to simply move through the womb of light and dark around us into who we are now, to be borne by the world into deepening life?

Groups oriented toward self-realization often include hugging as part of the conversation. When I went to college in the late 60s, I learned it was possible to hug male friends out of a deep appreciation of what we had gone through or who we were. (Handshakes just don't have the power of hugs.) In transactional analysis, we held one another, facilitating the inner dynamics of child, parent, and adult, mirroring the inner with the outer, feeling that risking the more primary levels of bodily energy was contained by the larger scope of the work. I remember how some people wept. Certainly, with some friends and with family members, hugging is possibly the only way to express our connection or appreciation of who they are. The actual energy is from before thinking, isn't it?—from a *mythos* that cannot be adequately (or efficiently) evoked by language.

When I hug another person, I am saying something from the way my blood is moving, from the solidness of my muscles and containing energy of my arms. I love to feel another person's arms around me, to feel our hearts beating, even for a moment. How strange it is to have a woman pull back her breasts so that we dance a herony ballroom waltz to Mozart a little, or to have a man go flat, like a door. Once I tried to hug a prominent poet after a poetry reading he had given. His poems and writings had been a part of my inner work for many years, and I felt I could express the importance of his presence in my life in this way. When I hugged him, he kept his arms at his sides and his chest went solid—I felt he was made of oak and rock. Perhaps he was communicating how his writing was something that passed through him, that as a creative artist he was like a door between the inner and outer. Perhaps I was confusing the situation. How difficult it must be to find oneself famous, to have men and women whose souls have merged with your own through the medium of art and community want to actually reach out and hold your body, to attempt to communicate something of their regard, and perhaps imagining the *mythos* of the art could possibly be marked by a mythic hug.

I remember how my grandmother hugged me. I was taken into her mammalian softness, into her strength and knowing. There was no hesitation, and I was lifted out of all conditions sometimes. I believe she channeled Earth Mother current, as I think back to how it felt. In her embrace I perceived that we were perfectly fine, beyond anything else. She had given birth often and had borne my father, and her joy was entirely open as she hugged me, her son's boy. She took me into her energy, giving me the gift of myself beyond words, beyond formalities, far beyond anything that was supposed to have been said. She often had tears in her eyes, and she was smiling, the energy open around us, through us.

We appear here together, are borne by one another, and return to our lives then, and keep going. Sometimes in a hug there is a primal or spiritual bearing, a first knowing of our species on earth, "a light around the body, through which the body moves" and is whole, but beyond even this, beyond all of this.

LENS

Tonight, warm in our bed,
we hold each other,
down in the flying sleep.
In the holding sleep,
I feel you pulling my earth
around you, where your earth
curves in dunes of sleep-
light, around us, with plants
and mammals breathing,
their violet and lit greens
swirling, and the rocks,
and showering snow outside
in the old earth,
and the lens of cells
watching a dawn!

Tonight the pine needles
are light from stars
of a first atom of sense
a person felt, and sun
through afternoon clouds
that the pines tower with
invisibly over us now,
with every small thing,
our shoes near the door,
the wheat bread, Mary's plates,
their sun of the dark
ground of light carrying us
through the veins,
night where our deep bodies
stayed rooted, and wake
themselves in time
into the world.

MOUNTAIN SNOWFALL

The snow falling
heavily onto the trees

is a light they carry.
Music from the radio

goes on, falling,
in the Bach canyons.

This floating
of the mountains

of snow, down
around the cabin,

brings chords
of the pine, junco,

blue jay, and takes
them, back into Celtic

pipes, crystal
floating with souls

of horses, and space
is heavy with days

we bring. And what
we are becoming

is light, that the trees
carry, and the snow

outside calming us.
Nowhere I can think of

would I go now.
No one I have become

takes me away
when I am with you

RADICAL NATURE

After months
away from the coast,
I see rock
lifting itself
from the foothills,
I see whales
diving down into the earth
of their ocean,
into the light
of their planet,
in the massive rock
becoming
their bodies.

This is a possible way,
as are cactus gardens
whose spirits
bring offerings
found between us,
like a spoon
or a wooden chair.
Or the glowing marks
of a mandala
in the armor
of beetles,
the wait of the owls,
the skies of dusk
hung between
years of talking,
in the accent,
or color of George's hair
when he speaks.

Tonight I stand
near the waves,
near their roar,
their coming into being,
their starlight
that sitars sound like,
that grounds
the green fire
in seeds, from inside
trunks of willows,
the moss-covered stones
in a month, the rose's
ultraviolet
asking.

Around 1840, Emerson wrote
that "we find ourselves...
reverently... before
the secret of the world,
there where Being
passes into Appearance
and Unity into Variety."
He saw that "nothing walks,
or creeps, or grows,
or exists" that is not
"exponent" of our "meaning."

And any sun
coming through
the way wood is shaped,
or fathering
the maple carries.

Any forgiveness
of the ant
on the slice of bread,
or whale
from the first time.
Any lake bottoms
that fish show,
hieroglyphic,
in chestnut-shaded
pulsings.

Any newly born sky
or glowing water,
any alley smoke
behind the oranges,
or mushrooms
behind houses
in wave-lifted
streetlight,
or snow falling
a squirrel feels
miles away
in the wind.

ᕙᕗᕙ

Drawing on life of living
  clustered points of light spun
      out of space
hidden in the grape.

—*Gary Snyder*

ᕙᕗᕙ

The centers of stones need your prayers.

—*William Stafford*

RESTORING SIGHT

THIS MORNING I WOKE, stood up, and walked to the kitchen. The lights worked, water poured from the tap, the floor was solid, the coffee smelled like rich soil. Outside, the ground was soft and permanent. The sky was above the earth. The supermarket was there, at the corner. The laundromat was dimly glowing with its cracked window. The bridge over the river was still over the river, and mostly I didn't see it. Mostly I took my life and earth around me for granted.

A month after the winter solstice, it's true—the days are widening, expanding in energy. The silver glow meets our desire to wake, earlier each morning. The change is slow, of course, the way hair grows, the way firs carve more breath into the sky.

At work, how much of our sense is channeled into the root hairs of details; how much seeing-power is drained into chores? I like moments when a person enters the room and we talk unexpectedly, or when a strange word flies onto the roof of the next building with a sea gull. I like the brief releases between the sounds from the printer when the color of someone's sweater glows through the window, or when I notice the postcard of the brown pelican flying.

As people move down the hall, they are surrounded by extra perception. Glances into rooms, faces seen for a moment, boxes, sheets of paper, words resonating in memory, dashes of crimson in the painting, blue sky in a window—so much at once fills where we go, how we move, what we think. Our senses have a lightning summarizing power.

At the eye clinic, patients are helped into the lobby, some able to only see indistinct shapes around them, some with debris floating through the images they see, some feeling a part of the roundness we take for granted closing in darkly. How would it feel to register trees as hulks and smudges, to know their trunks lead to branches but only see them enter an indistinct ceiling? Sudden breaks of unfamiliar sidewalks might be curbs or hoes left out by the grounds crew. The sound of a Pontiac rumbling half a block away might be suddenly terrifying.

If I were losing my eyesight, I wonder if it would be like walking through a cavern slowly becoming darker, like moving through more and more solidness, back into some kind of mountain. Would people I know seem to be sliding away from how I sense them? I can only imagine how dependent on others I'd feel. I realize how the way I see integrally creates my sense of being a person.

At the eye clinic, the physicians have studied their subspecialties to the limits of what is presently known. They are confident about what they can do, generally, or realize when they can't help a patient. In the past couple decades, the retina specialists have harnessed ways to reattach loose retinae, using futuristic LaSag Microruptor II YAG laser machines to burn hundreds of microscopic points into the tissue, fusing it back down into the eyes. They arc the burns around the retina into zones of the clockhours. The hour welds back into the person's soul a little more. Vision improves.

There are operations that open viscous membranes, procedures that reestablish the internal pressures of eyes, and diagnostic measures that outline exactly where structural problems exist, as fluorescent dye leaks in microseconds from tiny breaks. Ultrasonic graphics explore hidden topologies, and the systematic trial of lenses and magnifiers pinpoints existing potentials. The problem is almost always diagnosed; the people's eyesight is often partially restored.

For people whose failing sight cannot be surgically adjusted, technicians at the eye clinic find additional lenses, telescopes, and lamps so they might be able to read a few words or see if the burners on the stove are turned off. There are visors with lamps that can be worn, perhaps similar to helmets miners wear, and closed circuit television can be used to enlarge images into range. Of course, this is expensive, but how much more expensive it is if the people who could be helped are left to the continual care of others.

Perhaps those of us with eyesight are also like miners as we move through our days and look for what we care about. Is there a darkness even in light, answered only by our ability to perceive things more deeply? Of course, when we think about it, we know how much we ignore.

How must it feel to take a person into a laser room, to bend over her face and look into the workings of her eye? I know how I feel sometimes looking at the face of a sunflower blossom, at the seeds grown along their spiral unfoldings, the fiery yellow petals, the brown-yellows, the ignition of its form. The eye, too, spirals into its shape in the womb and moves through its curves and blossoming, and connects to the force that brought life into action, to the lightning that intelligently continues to genetically unfold.

In earlier centuries, mathematicians felt the underlying laws of form connected to profound beauty. The unity of the central life-giving impulse didn't just divide into things but an unfolding of geometric proportions. Often leaves circle around their stems revealing this inner spiraling. Seeds fill the face of the sunflower from within this impulse, and iris cells turn into their shape and allow light to curve into our being, as our inner light meets and replicates the world's light in the eye.

The Greeks studied the spiral generated from the proportions of the Golden Mean, and aesthetically felt its proportions produced the most pleasing shapes we might see. The human face, length compared to width, averages the Golden Mean. A series of numbers whose ratios approach the golden Mean proportion as they approach infinity—the Fibonacci Series—is another part of these dynamics. In "The Measure of Difference" (*Parabola*, Winter 1991), Robert Lawlor explains that the Fibonacci Series "governs… the laws involved with the multiple reflections of light through mirrors, as well as the rhythmic laws of gains and losses in the radiation of energy." It is a pattern "superimposable on the foetus of man and animals," a deep generative beauty within many things we can see and also within the process of seeing itself.

When I consider how much of what we perceive is through

eyesight, I can only imagine what would be lost if we couldn't see. When we look at the world, we take in surfaces, cross-modify their implications and designations, and witness a three-dimensional place. Further, we take the three dimensions and see into processes and association and experience additional dimensions. Lawlor describes the power of the spiral as integrally hinged on "transformation: what was a linear accumulation suddenly becomes a square, a surface, a plane. There has been a leap of growth." Intrinsically, seeing works in this way, integrating geometrically, beautifully.

I think of the people who are referred to the eye clinic. How afraid some must be, how distracted from what they might care about, how dependent on our knowledge of medicine they are. Thirty years ago, fewer could have been helped. Three hundred years ago—to be sure, it was a darker world if your eyes started to go bad.

I wonder what having lost one's sight would do to a person's dreams. Would they become a way to still live in the daylight world? Certainly, sound, voices, and music would take on added power. Is it possible to let that happen a little, anyway, even if we can see? How can I honor each of my senses more fully? How much of each day do I take for granted?

A LIGHT USED TO PERCEIVE

I.

A wind comes from the nuclear bombs
in our dreams,
but it barely moves the leaves.

A ship passes slowly with its ropes of light
fanned out into those watching it.

Back where the gulls roost,
forty feet below, the beach fills its lungs
and empties, exhaling.

Nothing is asleep.

II.

Nothing is asleep because the ocean is awake.

A workshoe appears in a dream.
A star over a night waterfall visits
through the acupressure.

A person asleep dreams with the light
she uses to perceive.

Ultraviolet shore rocks bank up
and loosen the waves.

III.

Blackberry vines crawl from the ridges.
Abandoned cars smolder
near the unreachable fruit.
Marbled resolutions
are chiseled by the way light flows.

Navajo rugs bring a lightning from saddles,
a loosening of morning grasses,
a center of the room.

A person awake sees
with the light he uses to dream.

TWO FOR THE INVISIBLE WORLD

I. *Scent of Garlic*

Huge carbon tree inside the universe.

Its mountain ravens fly over the hikers.
A drop of its dew is all the oil
that is burning.

Slender Wall Street clerks
wear its black turtlenecks in the evening.

One of its Rothko paintings
is the edge of dusk
and beginning of a Colorado snow,
a buffalo's belly heat in the valley.

The tree reaches out until its fruit forms.
It reaches further into the cribs
of sunken ships.

The scent of garlic roasted in oils
finds its way around the house.

II. *Three Sea Lions Fly In*

From the hedge, a cricket
makes a field that pulses but doesn't move.

It's an amber light inside his body
we can hear through the air.

Months out, at its perimeter,
it's a necklace of darkening blue
crystal and white grasses
for the tigery man.

There is a sound of light from the sun
reaching into the planet,
the movement of earth through pulsing
healing power, that the cricket
sings to the wound, to the night.

The faces of three sea lions
fly into a person's chest.

DREAM TRAVEL

I.

ONE NIGHT, after an intense acupressure session the evening before, I dreamt Marilyn showed me a magazine article about an especially authentic plaza of small shops in a few brick buildings from the turn of the century. The area had modestly thrived through the years and only recently had been discovered by the rest of the city. Immediately, my dream teleported me there, into the middle of a closed-off brick street between the old buildings by the river. Though it was about 10:00 p.m., a number of the craft shops and galleries were still open. I sat in the courtyard with a few old men watching a slow-moving televised news program on a small TV set. Behind the television, a block away, was the Willamette River, and overhead, the night sky. We sat quietly, far apart, anonymously, relaxing after the workday.

One of the men finally decided to leave, and I was astonished as he turned to wave goodbye to the rest of us. We waved back and one of the men told him to take it easy. I realized a comradery had developed between us, though we had barely noted one another's presence while we watched the news. But watching the news in this old part of the city, with the night river in the background, with the night stars overhead and warm glowing markets and cafes nearby, had connected us. I realized I knew that the man leaving had been traveling through Portland and had found this place to rest before returning to his hotel. Like him, I had come to this place where travelers rest. Part of the acupressure I had experienced the night before involved work on the triple warmer, the calm center, and this dream decided to take me into a place that reflected a protected openness and calm.

This was certainly the way to watch television!—outside, under the night sky. The old men in the dream knew that it is okay to just sit at the end of the day, if that's what you want to do. Some dreams like this lead down into their scenes and people; other dreams want to keep moving. In one sequence from a while ago, I had returned to the home where I was born. Perhaps forty feet behind the house I could see a large hill, and noticed that the lower three or four feet of its base was molten wax. It was my job to help control a dog, cat, and bird in the backyard, keeping them near the house. But there wasn't much light, and suddenly one of the animals slipped into the wax. Then I could see the entire hill was made of something like molten wax and was melting from inside out. Terrified, I shouted the dog's name, but he slid down entirely into the hill. Then the other animals also slipped and were swallowed up by the wax. The poor animals—so hard to control, and certainly not deserving this. I felt sorrow, for them, but in the dream I also sensed that it was possible they weren't actually dead. Perhaps they were just changing their physical form. Would they re-emerge from the shape-changing energy of this hill in different bodies? Clearly, the context of the dream had broken away from time, and traveling to this primordial place of beginnings and changes, it had asked me to wake a little.

II.

On another night, another traveling dream took me back to beginnings. I had climbed a huge pole at a construction site and was able to interview a worker about what it was like being so high off the ground all day. He looked like a calm and reasonable George Schultz (who used to be with the Reagan administration), and said that, yes, it was important not to lose track of the work and look down. Apparently, we were in part of a three-year job training effort, working on gigantic silos in Africa. Workers had to spend long hours twenty stories above the ground on flimsy scaffolding. Schultz told me we shouldn't forget that even though we are this high and the animals on the ground look tiny, that many are elephants angry about what we are doing. This was shocking, so

I climbed down to the first floor to get a better view of the elephants.

The room at the bottom of the silo was cool, with a concrete floor, and became the garage of my parents' house when I was ten. I didn't see any elephants but could feel their presence through the walls. I noticed the back door was a foot open and fearfully wondered what wild animal might have gotten in. I walked to the living room and saw the feathers of blue jays and English sparrows all over the floor and began to moan and cry. I followed the feathers down the hall to the bedroom of my parents. The cat had eaten the birds there. I wept and waited for the boss to come in and tell me what to do, or take some of the grief away from me, I guess. This woke me up.

I don't read this dream as an inditement of my parents, but on some level, the place where I had been conceived was where the violence happened. From the scaffolding, this couldn't be seen— from the momentum of our technology. But back on the ground, was this dream showing that a major horror of having been born in a time of rampant population growth is the slow destruction of other beings on the planet? The cat was a family member, and his actions represented what we are doing to the natural world? From the construction site, this dream traveled to Africa, and then to where I came from, emphasizing the larger context, pointing to how we are trapped here in the earth's struggle and wide-spread destruction. The anger of the elephants is part of us. The cat and bird feathers are part of us.

III.

Some details travel from distant places into the molten energy of dreams. In one dream, I walked through a large building ten floors high, trying to find my friend's apartment. After searching a while, I realized from the display cases that the building was a museum. I felt unhooked from the present year somehow, and noticed that the windows were unlike any I had seen. The floors sloped up two feet and seamlessly became immense windows, creating the illusion that the walls didn't exist. Everywhere I looked, the outside world seemed to be an extension of the museum. I worried about actually falling out of the building. But this architecture was certainly tuned to the energy in much of the art, balanced between openness and risk, vision and virtual containment. The museum had been constructed to emphasize the wild edge of the art it preserved.

As I walked down the 10th floor hallway, it occurred to me that this was the new Denver Art Museum. The guards were animated, many in their late 20s or early 30s. A couple guards approached me to let me know it was closing time, and from the way they talked I felt something was different about them, that they were young in some new way. I asked what the year was, and they said 2052! I stood in my 1987 body, excitedly explaining that apparently I had stepped into some sort of warp and had traveled through time. One guard was interested, and a man near her joked about the experiments going on in another part of the building, that apparently they had turned up the juice again and had had some peripheral leaks. My presence there was part of this overflow. I couldn't believe it, 2052!—I didn't think human culture with its nuclear arsenals would survive that long.

While talking with the guards, I tried to take in as much as I could. I told the woman that people looked generally the same as in 1987, with no mutations, but she quickly replied I hadn't seen so and so—I couldn't understand the syllables of the name. As we walked to the elevators, which were more like light tubes than solid rooms on cables, I saw carved cupboards from the 20th century that seemed to be inspired by Blake and Native American symbology. We looked at objects from daily life sealed in showcases. On a desk by the curator's office, a photograph of Edward Abbey had been framed and signed by the president of the "A.A.S.P.C." I had the sense that not only had culture survived but that the back-to-earth movement had become a major force. Near the electronic gate by the elevators was a sloppy joe stand, where the sandwiches were made from rice, tofu, and black beans. The guards sarcastically joked about the food, but it looked good to me.

Then I met the husband of the one guard. He was handsome and strangely glowing—she introduced him to me as one of the mutations I had wondered about. He was striking in stature and beauty—square, sensitive, his eyes deeply alive. I was struck by everyone's good humor and nonchalance. It was a wild, hopeful dream—the Denver Art Museum in 2052! The specifics of this dream were so clear, I woke wondering if it had been an actual experience. What kind of television will exist in 2052? Will it create virtual reality and move through the cosmos in ways we can't imagine? What did the city look like? How difficult it is to look ahead that many decades, with overpopulation, destruction of natural resources, and the possibility of nuclear war part of the picture. I realize how blocked my sense of 2052 usually is. Do we actually trust civilization as we know it will exist by then? And if we have trouble imagining 2052, how does that affect our art and daily energy?

IV.

In another dream with many details, I began working as a janitor in a building, when I heard Bill T.'s low baritone laughing. As always, he was sharing intense poetic ideas with students near him. I walked up to a powerful young poet in his class, wanting to explain how much I appreciated the depth of her images, the emotional rootings, and dimensions, but she seemed so young and was bewildered by the praise. Apparently praise interrupted her process, so I pointed to others who were working in similar ways. Ted L. was one of those people, and it turned out that he was to fly in later that day. We had stepped outside, but an extraordinarily hard rain began. Then I saw Ted out in the rain, as he had just flown in. We stood beneath a smooth yellow-trunked tree, some kind of willow. You could feel the tree's power, and its beauty.

As the rain calmed down, I could see Ted was wearing a carpenter's belt, strung with all kinds of tools. He was ready to work, was intensely serious, as if it were morning at a construction site. We went into an old house where he was going to make a new room on one wing of the first floor. I knew it would be something I had never seen before.

So the dream had traveled. Inside the house, I found myself working on a paper with a friend who felt like my neighbor when I was little and then became John B. Together we worked on a paper titled "Radiation, The Radiation of Art, Genetic Strengthening, and Genetic Growth." I believe this was the title. The paper was already quite long and detailed, and we were under contract with a major magazine that was a cross between *Harper's* and a wild arts magazine. The point of the article was to establish the connection between what radiation does to genetic structure and what experiencing strong art does to a person. We edited and revised the paper for weeks, and fit the text to vividly dynamic graphics. That is, suddenly it felt like we had been there working for weeks.

The morning after the dream, I noted that the first part of the paper established certain laws of radiation and then slowly worked to document what kind of healing or nurturing radiation art makes. Our argument felt quite clear, and we were convinced we could present to the general public *proof* of what art does for the soul and why our society should not only allow its growth but fund it heavily. The paper included demonstrations of vibrational levels, color harmonics, and resonance of multiple themes. The radiation in art came, however, from inside the person experiencing the art as much as from the art, so we had to measure with sensitive instruments.

Included in the paper were case studies, analyses, extended comparisons, group studies from other countries, paragraphs that intensely demonstrated the varieties of inner nurturing fields ("in the Realm of the Possible," John noted). Then the paper tied the art radiation in with stronger genetic biases, more powerful immune systems, and highly attuned offspring. We took our time, but felt compelled to finished the project. At one point in the dream, we were interrupted from the hall by a nurse who was also a writer, telling a female patient who was glad to have given birth that the baby was premature and that she would need to take the baby back inside until it was ready. Apparently, it wasn't a complicated process to hook the baby back up through the umbilical cord, and to then wait for the right time for birth. We became more intent on documentation after that, working up appendices of artists and their ranges of healing radiation.

Suddenly I was reviewing the appendices we had completed. In Appendix 12, we had listed Paul Simon, Bob Dylan, and Jimi Hendrix, among others, in a study of popular music, and then learned that Simon and Dylan would be doing an album together. I became excited and wondered if Hendrix would perform with them, as well. John looked at me and said he didn't think so—since Jimi is *dead*. The finality in his voice, and the tenderness, stressed the importance of my realizing Hendrix is gone, and yet gave me room to have made such a mistake. In the dream, I saw I had confused living as a person with living through one's art, and yet living as a person includes spontaneous unknowns and breakthroughs and sensitivities that could only be eluded to or captured in art. This was at the heart of our study, that art can embody the spontaneity and health of our deepest life. But the realization that Hendrix was indeed dead drove home how unique our time is, our minutes together, as they are measured in exchanges, in perceptions, in deep feeling and communion, and in the *work*.

I woke from the dream with all these details and with the sense that the old house was a thriving center for the exploration of connections between art and science, work and nurturing, and body and spirit. It was also a cottage industry and not part of a corporation. That morning, Marilyn told me an image from one of her dreams, that our birds were singing and suddenly a radiant goldfinch landed on the window sill, trying to get in. He and the birds in our house talked together through the window, and he was luminous, like sunlight, a golden bird wanting in.

Some dreams go to the window. Some travel to distant places through the medium of their shape-changing energy, speaking what they deeply know. Space is sometimes bridged by a force field, the way art glows with its transformative radiation into the next century. Some dreams look profoundly into birth and grief, and some speak by traveling, though where they take place a golden bird wants in like sunlight.

EVENING

AFTER WORK, the evening moves like a tide into the
neighborhood, filtered through the slow-burning lights of houses
and streets. It breaks open in its currents the way light strikes film
in a camera, all at once, more than we know, more real than we
imagined, carrying the scent of the ocean it comes from, asking
softly from behind the parts of our lives. Down the road, not far
away, a few friends are talking. Energy is moving. Evening extends
who we are.

I know how easily daylight supersedes all this, how
sometimes the afternoon streamrolls, how our desire to find out
more than we know keeps us seeking further light, and yet this
evening I want to simply let what is entering extend its ancient tide,
its moment now, where we are. Wrapped by this letting go, this
balancing, breathing, the calm evening, it is possible to sit in the
body and go back, to places, and past them, further back, into the
body earlier. In the unfolding of senses and scenes, I sit back into
the boy, and younger—back—and want to say I can feel how being
carried by my mother felt, being lifted up into her arms and taken
to bed.

I lie down on that bed, and see the house around me in
Ohio, and feel the wind and night over the town, and imagine
myself still younger, back through gates of the evening air and sky
with stars and clouds, back into my smaller body. I am lying on the
bed, picked up by my mother, given to my father, and put back, and
the light is turned out, except for a small night-light, and the door
left open a bit to the hall. I lie back into my body, when almost
nothing had happened yet, and still the energy is around us and
through us. I fall asleep, wake up crying and am held and then put
back down, and fall back into sleep there.

We have this sense in our bodies. It is possible to go back
further I want to say, and feel my body now—my chest, lungs, my
arms, my legs and feet—back through the evening, through my

mother. I am floating in her, in our warmth. Her blood enters mine. I am going to be a boy. I am wrapped by her full moving body. It is evening. I feel myself folded, unfolding from the coil of my energy in her. We know where we are, and I want to go back further, past when I knew my form, down into my body before I became a boy, only weeks after it started. Years were in those weeks, unfolding, I think now. The vast evening held us. I feel my body as potential, neither male nor female, but human, forming, as who I am now.

If I sit at my desk on a Wednesday evening and say I feel friends through the distance, I think my prebirth body is partly sensing this. I feel from all around me and know there is a shared blood, still, deep in human synergy. The evening is the mother's body around us and has always been around us, and will always return, and sometimes we see her, and when we leave daylight forever, she will still be around us. The preborn body knows this, feels this, around the body in the light and dark flowing of being an adult. The evening carries us as we sit here, and sometimes her love can be felt, her love for the life inside her that she is holding.

I walk down the hall to the kitchen, and then return here, listening. Rain at the smallest pores of the fir roots threads into their veins, steadying the old needles, and shining darkly through the yards. Ducks are moving together beneath the low branches at the edge of the marsh. In a nearby cat's body, four cats are beginning to take their shapes, their eyes and brains forming, their paws and spines. How this earth began to form shows up in ways our hands move, how our minds look from deeply within us.

I want to remember the prebirth body in each person I see. I want to see the boy or girl around 8 or 9, and then witness the adult carrying heaviness that comes with the years and hear what the person is saying, and know who the person is that I could never know, that I can keep asking for in how I listen. Though daylight speeds everything up, the evening gives us each day, and carries the form we have taken for this life, and returns to us in her tide from behind everything, sometimes with stars, the moon, or clouds in the night sky.

IN LATE MARCH THE FROGS SING THROUGH THE WALLS AND TREES AT LA MORTICELLAS'

On Johnson Road
  the frogs are singing
  in thick chickeny voices,
  belching lizard winds
  croaking through the soil
  in their throats, the soil
  that they slept in.
Through the window and walls
  their singing comes.
A door opens in the iris.
The old fern rows toward its bay
  at the edge
  of what it sees.
The dozens of frogs
  are singing after the rain
  beneath the moon of the firs,
  the moon clearing the sky,
  the moon holding still
  in its eggs pouring over the ground
  by the foamy mud that is waking.

They are singing to each other,
  to the roots of the trees,
  to the tiny unformed larvae,
  and to the jet that flew
  over the question,
  to the unfinished room
  of the house, they are singing
  as far as a leaf reaches

into its bird, like footsteps
of fir needles in the colosseum
of planets, like golden brown doors
in the rain voices, like
some forestry of moss,
they are singing into the rings
of wood, into the cores
with dark evening light
lit by amber.

On the road out of town,
    on the road through the atoms
    each piece of light knows
    and collects with its lives,
    through the pinecone's sadness,
    through the white feathers
    brushing the new bank buildings
    silently, the frogs are croaking
    and belching the mud-masks,
    as they impregnate the peppers
    and asparagus, and set loose
    blue-violet fires with a brush
    of a branch on your cheek.

The frogs are singing from the basement
    of soaked leaves, from the iridescent wax
    on a lamb-fly's tongue, from the sweet
    sweet honey that loves us.
They sing like granite holding steady,
    they sing with old animals
    in our bodies, and with new grass,
    with the evening, as we sit
    at the thick wood of the table,
    and talk together for hours
    by the wide-awake pond.

WEDNESDAY MOVING
THROUGH WEDNESDAY

IT IS WEDNESDAY EVENING on the planet moving through
space. It is something happening moving through Wednesday
before anything goes on. It is $161.96 before it is an egg breaking,
before the sun is lima beans cooking, where Wednesday is combing
through hair and streets of Wednesday.

Actually it isn't just space, of course, but an intricate matrix
of pull and release, orbits and oblong trajectories, and on the ground
are home tables, feathers, photographs of 1983, the new letter of
love, the fiscal robin calls on a form, the gazelle speeds of nylon for
the olfactory, the scent of ginger, the stove a medieval altar, the sun
setting over the table and chairs, Wednesday moving through
Wednesday.

My friend R. says it is energy that all is and moves through,
and that ambient energy can be tapped through a device he and a
few others are working on, thanks to the help of two psychics in
Montana, I think it is. They are mystics talking into our mysticism
of numbers and objects, looking for a home in 2038, looking for
completion in the hour of earth now. And so R., an engineer for HP,
is working with physicists he knows in other cities, trying to
construct a prototype of the ambient energy machine. Now, that
would change things.

So it is ambient energy the planet moves through and is,
energy moving through energy, heart through heart fields, night
through night, morning through morning. All that our words have
been building moves through our words. It is earth here, where
we do a few things, ambient rain falling in the rain, energy in the
stillness falling in the stillness. Relativity makes its Oregons, not far
from the ocean-speaking, not far from workweeks so close to 6:30,
so immediately rain and light of earthiness, Wednesday of our
hands and feet, Wednesday of each other.

A bark beetle chews more hieroglyphic tunnel in the Doug
fir. A Buddhist lama steps through the lobby with an aura of

people. A friend lifts another Rainier in the amber light, as herons fly singly over the Willamette before the last of dusk, the garlic and earth scent combing faint waters. A bus drives over the bridge, flanked by cars and houses, by unseen rails and turns of leaf light reconstructing it constantly in a Wednesday.

A person makes money, and everyone else has given it to him. A crow wakes up over the lost bread. Our actions are taking place into the place, a few sea gulls over the sudden car light of a sentence. The planet breathes, mostly not human of course, soil holding the firs, the worms scrolling darkly through rooty past tantrums, plankton foaming in pillows of a taciturn bay, baby raccoons mewing down through sticks of uncollected numbers, and clothing still used past its catalogued shapes. There is this softness in used bills, in faint silvery green pushing carts behind the moon.

A person breathes, and everything has given it.

So money is mostly firs and blackberries, and hair on forearms at the table. It is a look from a person in the hallway, sidewalks of looks, swelling up in a mist around the small denominations. If you put your nose in a bowl of coins, it might smell like the side of the car, or like rocks hot from the sun, or like bitter soil where the raccoon pissed, but dogs know more about this. Birds, too, have a perspective we can only intuit from how they move in the fast light around them.

Sometimes we become accountants on a Wednesday, explaining a car or a few rooms, outlining plumbing and outlets into numbers that drain behind walls of a bottom line. But don't ask me to explain more. The rock holds the soil and the sky holds our heads, and the moon lets the earth go beneath it. The salmon allow us to sit here, the way streetlight breathes and grass speaks for a billion ants outside any framework.

In the ambient Wednesday, our shoulders and faces appear from ancient sources. We talk and hours move through maple leaves, intensely, plainly, so much in faith moving through form, Friday re-entering its Wednesday, people moving through people moving until we step into the room together, dovetailed by cormorants, Wednesday given by the small cafes in Newport, Wednesday labored over in sweat shops in Mexico City, our hands worked into us by a woman in Bangkok, the sweater on loan from the Brazilian streetlight, the teeth and their fillings given over from European capitols on a day Wednesday gets to, the cars hovering of bees heavy rhododendron Nepal blood pulsing in the temples of an elephant looking this way, the wind from our engines, the askings, the curves of facial wholeness.

So this hour, this planet of raccoons and Wednesdays, the disguises carted in by nakedness, hair with its smooth skin, eagles with their billion ants and bedrock, money with its rusty softness a billfold holds. We are together, between things, where shapes open, where desire breathes the evening, where the people working at the harbor take a break a while near water lights and sky lights, the firs standing into the breath they help carve so slowly and clearly. There are shudderings of hatching wasps near the garage, papery nests with the scent of dollar bills and faint cat spray, news programs of dusk shimmering over a robin's egg, behind the passing train.

The way the woman with four children kept working after the father ran off threads a Wednesday. Sometimes there is no choice, patients touched by futuristic lasers welding their retinae back into their eyes, living rooms couched in cool flames of a Tibetan mandala a lama scoops up from the sand painting into the urn, honoring the passing of the sun and moon and stars. A small thing said is part of a fir, a forest of things said, the hour its ambient moving or not moving, something happening, nothing happening.

A few locust husks glow in the moonlight beside the nation.

A dollar bill folded or stretched open, touched by thousands, given by millions, is part of the breathing. The animals touch us with starlight. The night sky of Wednesday moves through its actual energy.

A SCENT OF BLACKBERRIES

IT IS AN EVENING after working, a quiet after the landscape, a hum in the stopped train, a river rushing, felt through the solid ground. It is an hour instead of a decade—this spring the planet turns back through—blood moving through blossoms of living tissue, breath fiery with towering Willamette firs where crows are resting back in cool syllables of things. It is a moment restless as the scent of a cut orange, silent the way Lovastatin sits on a counter, disassembled as a kayak with its parts all over the living room of a book out of print, our vision blurring from an 80s, our arms still wavering in ancestors' reaching.

When we sit together, we can feel it—the planet this spring turns back through—after the folds of a scarlet poppy decided to rest in cool wind passing through webs of starlight and cherry branches. When we listen to an owl's whooing we can't quite separate from the ambient river sound, sometimes we turn to see the bank of books behind us, the clauses in cell walls, the heavy fern slopes and machine shops of muskrats. It is an evening of part of the moon and part of the sun's deep diving.

It is the distance from a person's weight to the energy of *christos* that the river's earth moves with, that the light of some things shows in purple and yellow. It is an evening of soap from diamond rings near electromagnetic scans, barges of hospital wards drifting toward the delta of guitars, magazines launched into spectacular recovery of a curl of hair or smoothness of skin. Ideals hover over the ballroom floors that men or women spent some time on their knees for, as sea gulls leave their hovering in the air, as papers let loose wavering images of parts of ourselves. It is an evening after that, a flowing scan from beaver dens, gleaming with scars of streetlit cell walls, the night turtle swimming through our sense of the solidness.

The new buildings hover in their incomplete form, as part of the hour shuffles its immigrant silverware, and plates are lifted out of red dishwashers, steam swelling out of felt mechanics, bones throwing out their scent of blackberries. It is spring with an openness focused into mineral tunnels of active thought, openness that wildly jets around the turtle's shelled flying, flickering in the look from a man sipping coffee, in the configuration of violets on the poster from India.

In this soup, there is cedar after the workday, the engine allowed to free-fall through its energy, the rain allowed to wait in molecules of black and white cats, the locusts allowed to assemble in the voice box of a green apple, the old runes carried back into the cave of the white forecasts. There are bison painted on shadowy light as it falls through a lawn, ducks screaming through a stratosphere to where they sit on the slow water quietly, acorns full of bilge and rocking that hold their shapes far back in their impulses, in the green fire.

After the workday, the panels of voices are stacked by the garage, and hair falling gently over another's skin shows in mirror images. The moment of wood and rain hovers over us, exuding a scent of blackberries. It is an evening with wood all around, wood in its leaves breathing up into red-orange thresholds of Tibetan rhododendron shadows, wood ghostly and flattened into pages where light passes over the grain of a mountain desk, chairs and tables and woodwork and carved bird-people, masks that open from the raven into the earth goddess face, copiously, wooden, with open eyes. And the house is wood, the wisteria blooming in full purple clusters, fragrant, overflowing. In the evening wind, the house is a wooden flute back in the ambient noise.

A jet rumbles overhead in its surf, and late ocean light hovers holographically through tropical radios behind the blueblack air. There is surf from planets above us, the earth reaching out, extending its magnolia, its monarda, its forsythia, and the children who haven't arrived, the old people still in the future. There are names passed around like pollen, like tiger lilies, like Toyotas driven up to a glass window, TV complexes free-floating in rooms of chance as the hour holds through *mythos* of a body behind its particular senses, some of which are blackberry.

The thick vines sprawl and thread through tree limbs and hedges, as wooden pencils press down into the nest of a word. Numbers on patient charts begin to add up and then subtract down, the exercises from third grade sharpening their ginger. There are astral marigolds, desert violets of neon, the scent of wooden pencils like hearing a grandfather's voice in our hair, the inner skeleton guarding through its muscles and smoothness of moving, quietly, beneath things.

I want to say things moving between things. It is an evening when hydrogen of some daylight lifts off in steam from a few roads, when larch mountains of snow hold into their water, the waves still carrying ancestors not far away, the buildings someone imagined that were never built still almost nearby. It is an evening of peppermint and India ink and exploring rain, a river rushing, felt through the solid ground, the scent of blackberry around us. It is an hour of musk oil and a blue light and fresh celery and old windows reaching back through earth into the air.

THE NIGHT ENERGY
MOVES IN WAVES

I.

The solid night is also energy.
Potential hovers. Blue suns glow
in the night sky of each cell.

What are we giving up, that we can't
do without? The radio brings a dust
from Europe. Its ocean moves in waves,
carried by slower waves, and slower waves,
until they are solid. Its luminous fish
are like blue flames from another century.
Breathing, we give off a light
of salt and rainwater.

II.

What are the two lives we live?
Action and consideration, the ground
and air, the dragonfly eats
and turns, in a further life
of astral beauty.

III.

I have been waiting for things
to change, but they grow.
Each step deepens, then resides.
In the house, books swim back
under the vegetation. A koan
talks from the clocks of Monday.
In the storm, the seven bodies
bend in the grove of trees.

A frequency moves like wheat.
Steel glows in the yards.
Who has been telling us to do things?
Who can we love by sitting here, standing,
talking together? The music we love
passes through us like the whales.
For a few hours, our cells
move in that ocean.

ABOUT THE AUTHOR

JAMES GRABILL is the author of *The Poem Rising Out of the Earth and Standing Up in Someone* (Lynx House Press, 1994). Other books of poems include *To Other Beings* (Lynx House Press, 1981) and *One River* (Momentum Press, 1975). His poems have appeared widely in such magazines as *East West Journal, Inroads, kayak, Caliban, Poetry East, Another Chicago Magazine, NRG, Mid-American Review, Poetry Northwest,* and *High Plains Literary Review.* Presently, Grabill lives in Portland, Oregon, where he transcribes part-time at Good Samaritan Hospital and teaches writing and literature at Clackamas Community College. Also, occasionally he teaches "Writing with Light We Dream By" for the Oregon Writers' Workshop at the art school. Grabill studied at The College of Wooster, Bowling Green State University (B.F.A., 1974), and Colorado State University (M.F.A., 1988). He grew up in Bowling Green, Ohio, in the Eisenhower, Kennedy, and Johnson years.